THE FLOWER ARRANGER'S WORKBOOK

THE FLOWER ARRANGER'S WORKBOOK

Pauline Mann

Photographs by Derick Bonsall

B. T. Batsford Ltd, London

ISBN 0 7134 5945 X

Typeset by Deltatype, Ellesmere Port
and printed in Hong Kong

for the publishers
B. T. Batsford Ltd
4 Fitzhardinge Street
London W1H 0AH

Contents

Acknowledgements

Extensive thanks must go to Derick Bonsall for his calm, professional approach to all the photography; to Janet Hayton for helping with last minute displays and an array of minutiae; to Claudia Poland, Pauline's daughter, for overseeing the final stages of the book; and to Daphne Vagg for very generous and invaluable editorial help.

Early summer
There are many of the delights of early summer in this collection of garden material spiced with Lilium speciosum rubrum *and* L. longliflorum *from the florist. The paeonies are 'Sarah Bernhardt' and* P. officinalis *'Rosea-plena', the roses 'Zephirine Drouhin',* Viburnum tomentosum *'Mariesii',* Spiraea x vanhouttei *and a branch or two of philadelphus. The container is a shiny white bowl containing floral foam.*
(Arranger Jill Grayston)

Introduction

Flower Fashion

The way flowers are arranged in the home is as much a fashion as the clothes we wear, except that fashion in clothes changes more quickly. An 'in' colour often has only one season. Interior decoration alters more imperceptibly, though here also it is the way that colour is used that varies. Some people will always prefer the traditional in their houses just as there are people whose clothes fit in to the so-called 'classic' style. In a similar way, there will always be classic styles in flower arranging that we can rely on to return to when other possibilities become fads. Yet despite this, fashion in flower arranging has an important role, and change can bring refreshing vitality to bear on our flowers and house plants.

The Past

All civilizations have used flowers for ritualistic purposes, symbolism, medicine and food, and not until the seventeenth and eighteenth centuries were they painted in a manner that acknowledged the beauty of flowers themselves. Before this time they were merely decorations on a figure, often pagan or Christian, or simply adjuncts to the subject of the picture. It was the Flemish masters we must thank for their recognition and appreciation of a flower's individuality. Their grand flower-pieces appear to have inspired our Western mixed-flower designs that became popular towards the end of the Second World War. Articles in many women's magazines during Queen Victoria's and Edward VII's reign offered advice on flower arranging; several books were also written on the subject. In grand country houses the head gardener was responsible for the decorations on the dinner table, and although these were often made to last only a few hours, they could be very elaborate. In more modest establishments the daughters of the house might prepare the flowers, dotting the vases around in already overcrowded rooms.

A Flower Revolution

It was not until the late 1920s that Constance Spry brought fresh air into the art by using all kinds of foliage with her flowers, including hedgerow material and branches. She created large, loose designs that were startlingly different, and for some time her show cases were Atkinson's – the perfumer's – windows in Bond Street. The new age of flower arranging had arrived with Constance Spry, although it wasn't until after the Second World War that the style became a cult, giving pleasure to millions and culminating in the creation of the National Association of Flower Arranging Societies of Great Britain (NAFAS) in 1959. She was a genius at combining leaves and flowers that, at the time, other people would not have dreamed could be put together. Another part of her skill lay in choosing exactly the right container for the style of arrangement.

She became a legend in her own lifetime. Now much of her work appears dated, though there is never anything trite about it. She may have been responsible, in part, for our own geometric outlines, as she advised beginning by putting in the tallest flower or branch in the centre of the container and following this with the long horizontal side pieces – the beginning of a triangle, in fact. Now we are beginning to see a drift away from the somewhat overworked set designs, with their geometric shapes, which have dominated for at least the last twenty years. Today there is a yearning for more casual arrangements, and amongst the avant-garde, and in the very glossiest magazines, the trend has been towards grouping flowers in colour blocks. NAFAS has moved in another direction, exploring dried wood, seedheads, spathes and other strange shapes that combine to make sculptures out of plant material.

A display of pink gladioli in a low flat stoneware dish; the colours effectively pick up the background fabric and the stems reflect the floral backing design
(Arranger Pauline Mann)

The Japanese Influence

Although flower arranging only really developed in Britain in the twentieth century, the art was introduced to Japan in the sixth century by the Chinese. Japanese flower arranging, ikebana, has played an important part in this country, for the restraint practised by the various masters in using well-chosen plant material has certainly influenced our landscape and modern designs. The arrangements of those who have studied ikebana always have an extra, indefinable grace.

Seeking Supplies

Not everyone has a garden, and those who do may find it is too small for an endless supply of varied flowers and foliage. This means that most people are dependent on florist's shops or market stalls. The flower arranger should, with time and experience, become extremely selective and knowledgeable, seeking freshness, reasonable prices and a wide choice. Long-lasting qualities are desirable, too, but not if that means chrysanthemums for 52 weeks of the year, with never a sight of the seasonal beauties. The gardenless flower arranger must often make do with one bunch of flowers, but this is not always a handicap. It is very rewarding to have a vase of one sort of flower, as this really allows you to study and appreciate its characteristics. Bunches of one variety give good blocks of colour, too, whereas in a mixed arrangement some flowers may get lost amongst the whole collection.

Positioning Arrangements

Most of us have places in our houses where we always put flowers, and we don't vary these positions much. This is perfectly reasonable, for cut flowers need a stable surface on which to stand where they will neither be disarranged or knocked over. Wall vases are somewhat out of favour and fashion, perhaps because they limit the depth of an arrangement, but they can solve the problem for those short of space. One sizeable display makes a focal point in a room and is far more interesting than several smaller insignificant ones. This is a fashion we may have become used to but which is now changing slowly, mostly in modern surroundings, where you may find two or three related containers grouped together. The Americans call this linking of component parts *synergy*, from the Greek word *synergos*, meaning 'working together'.

As well as providing a highlight in a room, entrance or staircase, flowers will soften, or help to hide angular or unprepossessing features. Arrangements can be made to harmonize with a favourite picture or emphasize some well-loved ornament. The lighting of a group of flowers should not be left to chance – good effects can be achieved with little trouble. Flowers against a window will be silhouetted in direct ratio to the amount of light outside. Placing an arrangement on a low table in front of a window so that the daylight falls on it from above will show the colours at their truest. A plain wall makes a good background, but the wall colour should not be brighter than the flowers. An arrangement reflected in a mirror is attractive, and the mirror will reflect light as well as the flowers. Strong front lighting throws shadows on to the wall behind and side lighting helps to eliminate these. A light low down in front of a design will throw shadows on to a ceiling, which can give a marvellous effect in an otherwise dimly lit place. Unfortunately all ordinary electric light bulbs generate heat and should not be put too near to flowers.

Early summer
There is a definite Japanese flavour about the azaleas in the tall modern container against the drawn blinds. The colour combination is similar to that of the 'kanzan' blossom and orange tulips on p. 82 an example of adjacent colours made to bite. Mechanics – a pinholder.
(Arranger Sheila Addinall)

Summer

A modern interpretation of the 17th and 18th century Flemish style. The arranger has carefully avoided flowers of today's brash colours, which would have spoilt the polychromatic group. The original flowerpieces often contained flowers of all seasons, and showed the numerous bulbs and plants the Netherlands cultivated during this period. The blue and white container is reminiscent of Delft and so is thoroughly in keeping. Such a vase full would enhance any surroundings but it benefits from the plain background. Floral foam mechanics.
(Arranger Susan Holland)

Spring
A simple arrangement of lily of the valley in a white container. (Arranger Pauline Mann)

Common Light Sources

- Daylight: this gives colours their true value
- Ordinary tungsten light bulb: this shows reds and oranges well but makes blues recede; deep purples and dark blues will vanish
- White fluorescent lighting tube: this is good for blues and purples but turns reds and oranges brownish
- Candlelight: this is the least powerful of all. Arrangements made to be enjoyed by candlelight need white, tints or luminous flowers

Flower arranging is a very personal pleasure and one hesitates to give too much advice, but all suggestions in this book are made in the hope that you will enjoy the art of arranging even more if you experiment with form, texture and style as well as with the ever-changing kaleidoscope of colour and lighting. Foliage and flowering house plants are more popular than ever before, and the number of garden centres endorses this. Very seldom is there a home today without cut flowers or pot plants, so by being aware of their potential you can make maximum use of their attractiveness and wonderful colours.

Summer

If flowers are arranged with sufficient imagination and care a flower group may take the place of a picture and be the main object of beauty in a room. Pleasure is heightened when good lighting accentuates colours and textures. An exciting profusion of flowers from the garden in late September and the inclusion of Lilium 'Casablanca' from the florist provides a polychromatic crescendo at summer's end.

(Arranger Mattie Young)

1
A World of Colour

Many people find that a room devoid of flowers or plants is 'dead'. This can only be because plants are living entities, sharing with ourselves the mystery of inherited characteristics and a life span. Cut flowers are, in most cases, extremely ephemeral; this makes the enjoyment of them all the more intense. Flowers used as decoration give us the opportunity to indulge in many experiments, for the style of the room, its furniture and colour scheme all have to be considered. Arrangements can be of all shapes and sizes – delicate or strong, masculine or feminine, casual or studied in character – but as long as they are in harmony with their situation there is scope for endless variety.

Colour must be the design element that overall gives the greatest pleasure. Women, especially, have their favourite colours, and today it is fashionable to have one's skin tone analysed in order to find out the hues that are supposed to suit one the best. However, most people are happiest choosing their own colours to wear, and the same applies for interior decoration, where a scheme will be selected that makes the occupants of the house feel comfortable and at ease.

It is fascinating to evaluate colour, to place it in its various categories and to understand what happens in different lights and surroundings, for colour is never constant. It is also evocative, and will calm or excite, seem warm or cold, look heavy or lightweight; a design element with such power and variety is vital in life.

The Language of Colour

Fortunately, most of us are allowed to use colour as we wish. In our homes and with our clothes we can usually do exactly as we like – and it is a pleasant freedom. The following explanations of colour and its effects are well-tried theories used by artists, which are worth understanding and considering; they are only very general guides and not unbreakable rules.

The Colour Wheel

The pigment theory has a language of its own, which is demonstrated by the colour wheel on page 00. Once you understand it, it becomes second nature to visualize the depth and intensity of any colour being used or talked about. At a basic level, colours are divided into two groups: *chromatic* colours are those of the rainbow – red, orange, yellow, green, blue, indigo and violet; *achromatic* colours are not found in the rainbow and are known as the neutrals – white, grey and black.

Here are some useful colour terms

- The term *hue* distinguishes one colour from another, for example, the hue of yellow; the hue of blue; etc.

- The word *value* has been adopted to signify lightness or darkness. The *value* of a hue is changed when one of the neutrals is added: when white is added to a hue the result is a *tint*, when grey is added a *tone* results, and the addition of black makes a *shade*.

- The word *chroma* or *intensity* refers to the amount of pure undiluted hue present – i.e., it is the *strength* or *weakness* of a colour. *Chroma* is lessened by white or by the introduction of a neutral or another hue.

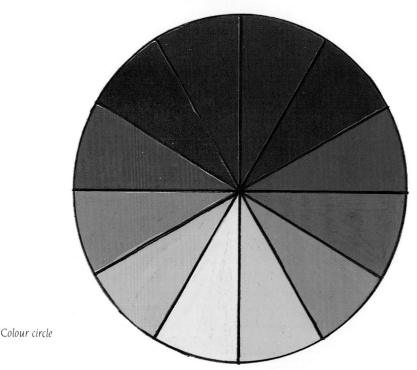

Colour circle

Primary colours are yellow, red and blue. It seems like magic that all the other chromatic hues can be mixed from these three colours.

Secondary colours are violet, green and orange. These are first mixes of the primaries:

red + yellow = orange
yellow + blue = green
blue + red = violet

Tertiary colours are made from the blending of a primary and secondary hue, first from one side of the primary and then from the other side of the same primary:

red + violet = red-violet
red + orange = red-orange
blue + green = blue-green
blue + violet = blue-violet
yellow + orange = yellow-orange
yellow + green = yellow-green

The permutations are limitless, as everyone knows who has examined the sample cards in a decorator's shop, showing all the mixes that can be obtained for the customer.

The first colour-wheel flower on page 17 has a centre of pure, fully saturated hues. Division one has had white added and has resulted in *tints*. Division two shows *tones* (grey added), and the tips of the petals demonstrate *shades* (black introduced).

The next colour wheel, page 17, is a simple example of *chroma*. The flower's centre is fully saturated whilst the subsequent divisions are progressively weakened with white.

Black, white, grey and brown

Do not dismiss black, white and grey because of their so-called neutrality. They are far too important, for they are the means whereby all the ranges of tints, tones and shades are produced.

Black really has no variations apart from texture, which does markedly alter its appearance. There are no black flowers, but it makes a dramatic backdrop both for strong and delicate colours.

Grey must be the acme of neutrality when it is exactly half-way between black and white. It is against grey that all colours are seen at their truest. However, the range of grey from the palest dove to gunmetal or battleship is extensive.

Value, tints, tones and shades

Chroma and intensity

White has a life of its own and is full of variations. The late Constance Spry considered the white cyclamen to be the whitest of all flowers. It is fascinating to note how the numerous petal textures change the quality of a flower's whiteness. A shiny petal will reflect the stamen colour, changing its own colour very slightly. There is also a category of greenish-white flowers, which are exceptionally beautiful.

White containers need all, or certainly some, white flowers in the design, as do white accessories, or the white is too dominant (see page 61). White flowers, to my mind, are at their best arranged on their own with foliage for contrast. If they are mixed with other colours these should be only tints, or the luminosity of the white dominates in the display and the white looks dotted about.

Brown is often thought to be a neutral, but it is actually a mixture of orange and black with a wide range of tints, tones and shades of its own, from palest beige to darkest chocolate.

Colour Harmony

Complementary colours lie opposite each other on the colour wheel. Opposites contain none of the other's hues, so the contrast is total. Examples are violet and yellow; green and red; orange and blue.

Monochromatic colour schemes are of one hue only, but they can use all the variations of both *value* and *chroma*. Such schemes are very restful.

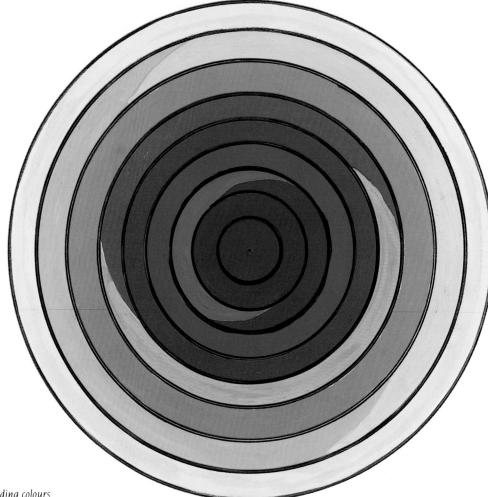

Advancing or receding colours

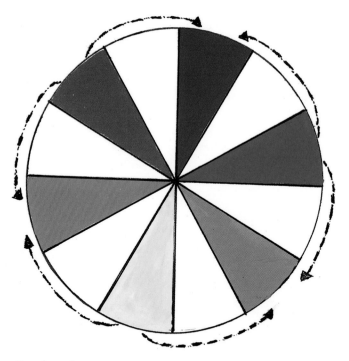

Secondary colours

Tertiary colours

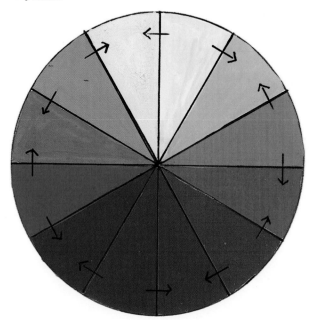

Polychromatic colour schemes include every possible combination of hues, polychromatic meaning 'many coloured'. In flower arrangements the best examples of mixed colour are the Flemish pictures of the seventeenth and eighteenth centuries. It is supposed that the much-loved arrangements of assorted flowers derive from these.

Adjacent or analogous colour schemes have a primary or secondary colour as a common parent and lie next to one another on the colour wheel. They are widely used in interior decoration. A look through any glossy magazine advertising fabrics and household goods shows rooms decorated in adjacent colours. More variety is possible than at first may come to mind, for there is the whole gamut of *tints*, *tones* and *shades* of the adjacent hues.

Triadic colours are those that are equidistant from each other on the colour wheel. Examples are red, yellow and blue; orange, green and violet; red-orange, yellow-green and blue-violet.

Impact

Some colours are vibrant, almost aggressive, others retire; some appear heavy and others lightweight; and then there are warm and cool colours. Here are the terms used to describe these characteristics:

Certain colours seem to be nearer to you than others. These are called *advancing colours*. Pure orange, yellow and red are the most advancing, green is said to be neutral, while blue and violet recede.

Luminous colours are those that stand out in a poor light. White is the most luminous of all followed by those containing a large proportion of white – the *tints*. Next is yellow, yellow-orange and yellow-green. Violet is the least luminous colour of all apart from black.

Some colours seem *lighter* or *heavier* than others, too. White and *tints* naturally seem lightweight. The *tones* – containing grey – heavier, and the *shades* that have black in their make-up, heaviest of all. Other colours can seem warmer or cooler. If you divide the colour wheel into two, the side containing red and orange is the warm side and the side containing blue and green the cool one. Yellow and violet take their warmth or coolness from their neighbours, for yellow appears cool against orange but warm next to green, whilst violet is cool against red but warm when compared with blue. This is an example of the inconsistency of colour, which is always affected by other colours as well as different light and surroundings.

2
The Primary Colours

Primary colours are usually thought to be too bold for small spaces; they need to be introduced with discretion in every situation – whether in the decoration of a room, fashion, garden planning or flower arranging. The simplest advice is to use the least amount of the strongest colour, and it is as well always to bear this in mind, for large proportions of fully saturated primary colour completely overwhelm smaller areas of softer tones and shades. Flowers of true primary intensity are not exactly difficult to find but there are fewer than might be supposed. In a polychromatic arrangement, too many flowers of full chroma make all the others pale in comparison. Similarly, if a pure hue is used in adjacent designs, then only a small amount is desirable, but full use should be made of all the tints, tones and shades.

Every arrangement needs some contrast and an area of greater importance or dominance. It depends on the style and mood of the arrangement as to how this is achieved. Modern rooms, with their lack of clutter, can take stronger colours and more contrasts than the more traditionally-furnished Western home. Therefore, the primary colours are usually kept for accent in the traditional design or used on their own in modern surroundings where space can play a part in accommodating them.

Red

Just as every flower has its characteristics of petal and leaf shape, so each colour has its own mood, effect and associations. It has been proved that red, for example, excites and quickens the heart beat, so it has become linked to the more dynamic things of life – in fact to life itself, as it is the colour of blood. It also stands for danger, revolution, passion and warmth. Such a colour can never induce feelings of restfulness but will always stimulate.

Characteristics

Red, in any tint, tone or shade, is an advancing, warm colour. If you choose to have red walls, they will create the effect of enclosing and protecting. The sense of protection will diminish as the strength of the red diminishes, until a very pale pink just creates the feeling of taking the chill off an otherwise white wall. Blue-red – even with only the slightest touch of blue – is heavier than the orange side of red; you have only to think of crimson versus terracotta to be aware of this. Consequently, the orange side of red is livelier and more youthful. Few colour schemes are as warm and inviting as this one, which can be broken up with pattern and a shiny surface or two to cool it a little. For accents, choose either a mossy green or bright orange. The former will also have the effect of lowering the temperature of the reds and pinks.

Types of red

Carmine – rich crimson-red pigment prepared originally from cochineal, the dried bodies of the *coccus cacti* insects, indigenous to Mexico and central America.

Crimson – strong, bright red tinged with purple (some blue is added to the red)

Magenta – brilliant crimson

Maroon – brownish crimson

Scarlet – brilliant red inclining to orange

Vermillion – brilliant scarlet

It is important to vary the depth of colour as well as the tints, tones and shades of red flowers. Tungsten lighting will enhance the reds and pinks; fluorescent lighting will turn them brown.

Red is traditionally a military colour, previously used for battle colours. Red is also associated with importance: the phrase 'red-letter day' derives from church festivals that were written in the Church calendar in red instead of black ink. In Victorian times, red was an extremely popular colour, partly owing to the invention of aniline dyes during Queen Victoria's reign. Many of the new trappings of the Victorian middle class were a deep rich red, leading to the phrase 'red plush', which symbolized the new standard of comfort.

Flowers

A flower that is a good example of primary red is the *Salvia splendens*, a great favourite in public gardens for summer bedding, and one which certainly makes a brilliant show. Other popular flowers that come in bright red and condition well (always an important consideration) are gladioli, carnations, tulips and gerberas. Needing more care are *Lychnis chalcedonica* and *Papaver orientale* (the oriental poppy), one of the most striking of all flowers because of its size, vividness and black petal bases. It was one of the flowers William Morris stylized in his wallpaper and fabric designs. Among today's silk flowers, the oriental poppies stand out, for they are the most realistic. The *Papaver rhoeas*, the poppy once common in cornfields, has a place in history, for it became the symbol of the armistice for the 1914–1918 war, commemorated annually in November. It was the subject of a well-known poem by a Canadian soldier, John McCrae: 'In Flanders fields the poppies blow between the crosses, row by row.' This little poppy isn't seen as much as it once was before weed control became so efficient, but it is extraordinary how many people cherish fond memories of it.

Foliage

I have listed some red foliage in Chapter 7. In the garden it looks well planted near grey foliage – but don't overdo either colour. Lots of new growth is reddish but like all new growth it is difficult to condition and is best seen growing rather than gathered. There are plenty of red-leaved indoor plants, so one may assume that red isn't all that robust.

For some time I pondered over how red leaves manufactured food, for this is a process carried out in the green of a leaf. However, a botanist assured me that the red pigment (contained in the cell sap) was only masking a plentiful supply of chlorophyll present in the leaf. One of the best red-leaved (in autumn) shrubs is *Cotinus coggyria*, the smoke bush. One variety, 'Notcutt's', has almost purple foliage with pinkish-purple inflorescences.

Modern roses

There must be a point where red-orange becomes orange-red, but it is difficult to identify. Plantsmen spend their lives experimenting with cross-pollination in an effort to produce larger, brighter, longer-lasting, disease-resistant, more highly-scented flowers of all kinds. It is the rose, however, that comes in for more than its share of commercialization. We are continually being bombarded with catalogues advertising yet another cultivar. The red-orange roses are the ones whose hues I like least, though this is a personal choice. It was brought home to me how brash the colours of many modern roses are when I spent the time visiting gardens that made a special feature of old shrub and species roses. The many different lacy foliages and soft colours made the modern orange roses look positively garish. Old roses are, of course, prone to mildew and other such horrors, and the majority flower only once in a season, sometimes throwing up a few second blooms, as a token effort. Nevertheless, I still prefer them; they win on scent alone, not counting their shapes, foliage and gentle hues. If you have only a small garden it is natural to want as much colour as possible, but there are many hybrid tea and cluster roses that come in subtle colours which are more attractive and less synthetic.

Wild flowers

Consider the tints, tones and shades of red: on one side are the flowers with blue in their make-up, and on the other those with yellow, the latter being the corals, apricots and peaches, darkening to terracotta, very popular today. The blue side of red is common amongst wild flowers: an apricot wild flower is almost unknown but mauve-pink ones are everywhere. I'm not sure that it isn't nature's favourite colour, though yellow must be a contender for this position.

Spring

Red isn't the commonest early spring colour but it is interesting to see just what there is as a change from spring's yellows and blues. There are many tulips, the red varieties of Chaenomeles japonica – sometimes known as quince – camellias and the young reddish foliage of Berberis thunbergii 'Atropurpurea'. This monochromatic design has been reinforced by a few florist's spray carnations and a stem or two of pink bergenia flowers. There is a plastic liner in the basket holding floral foam. (Arranger Pauline Mann)

Yellow

Characteristics

Yellow is the colour of sunshine and is equated with youth and joy. Nature is fond of it, and yellow is common in wild flowers. It is also a rich, special colour. In China it was used for the decorating of Buddhist temples and for the emperor's robes. In its gold form, it symbolizes wealth and royalty.

Flowers and foliage

In Great Britain, yellow is a winter colour as well as spring's most important hue, for it bravely begins to show long before spring's official beginning on March 21, owing to the winter jasmine (*Jasminum nudiflorum*), which starts to blossom in November. Next at the end of January the early aconites (*Eranthis hyemalis*) lift their green choir-boy ruffs that surround the yellow petals. Forsythia is everywhere, followed by masses of daffodils and early tulips. The whole countryside is slashed with yellow; many a garden, village green and roadside verge at the approach to towns and villages are planted with yellow flowers. We have become very daffodil-conscious people.

Like many of our spring bulbs, daffodils originated around the Mediterranean. Now they are widely spread, but it is interesting to note that none is indigenous to the Americas. As with the rose, the daffodil is constantly being 'improved' and a pink cultivar has resulted, which is not very attractive. Botanically, daffodils belong to the genus *Narcissi* and their family is the Amaryllidaceae. They form an enormous clan, which is divided into eleven groups and then sub-divided again. Some of the best are in division six, amongst the dwarf cyclamineus, 'Jack Snipe', 'Peeping Tom', 'February Gold' and 'Jenny': these have a delicacy of form and colour that is lacking in some of the larger ones.

Spring
Some of spring's yellows arranged in a basket. Against the blue background the yellow appears almost warm. The leaves used to give height are those of the Iris foetidissima, *a most useful thing to have in the garden for the leaves are strong and evergreen. The early double tulips are* Mr Van der Hoef, *which open to an almost paeony-like flower. The basket conceals a plastic box liner for floral foam, although tins for pinholders could easily be used instead.*
(Arranger Pauline Mann)

Summer

The earliest flowering climbing rose 'Maigold' is a rich, slightly coppery gold, holding within itself many tints, tones and shades. It is a rose that harmonizes with the colours of most baskets. The high handle encloses space attractively and this balances the flowing roses on the left. The basket holds a painted carton for floral foam.
(Arranger Pauline Mann)

The yellow Kaufmanniana tulip 'Chopin' is a soft yellow with a deeper yellow heart. Kaufmanniana tulips have enormous seed heads, which are excellent when dried. Another good early double is 'Mr van der Hoep', and I must also put in a good word for the cluster flowering tulips, their great charm being in the different-sized flowers borne on the long-stemmed clusters. When arranging it is such an advantage to have blooms of varied size. Later on, in May, I would miss the little *Allium moly*, whose seed heads are a clean cream and may be dried.

Early summer seems somewhat devoid of yellow, but it comes again in great strength with daisy-like August flowers. There are roses, of course, and 'Maigold', the climbing rose that always comes out first, is such a warm, coppery yellow, though it is not a repeat-flowerer like 'Golden Showers', which is a much shriller yellow. So it is the herbaceous border that carries on the yellow theme, with coreopsis, anthemis, heliopsis, inula and rudbeckia, along with yellow gladioli and dahlias. Many yellow dahlias are extremely acid in hue and those bordering on the orange side of the colour wheel are far more attractive. September is the true chrysanthemum season; the flower shops and markets have mixed bunches standing outside, and if there are any dahlias near it is easy to see how strong is the intensity of these compared to the muted chrysanthemums, though the yellow chrysanthemums are stronger in colour than any others in this genus.

Blue

Characteristics

Just as red and yellow are lively, advancing and exciting colours, the third primary is calming. The racing heart, stimulated by red, quietens in blue surroundings. Hospitals are often decorated in blues and greens for these very reasons. Blue is a colour associated with loyalty and purity.

Flowers

It isn't easy to pinpoint a flower and say that it is 'pure blue', but I believe the spring-flowering *Gentiana acaulis* and the autumn-flowering *Gentiana sino-ornata* qualify. Cornflowers (*Centaurea cyanus*) are also an intense blue. These small flowers used to be a companion of the field poppy (*Papaver rhoeas*), both growing amongst the corn until modern cultivation exterminated them. The Tudors loved the cornflower and introduced it into their gardens. In Gerrard's *Herball* of 1597 it is called 'Blew-Bottle'. Anchusa and many delphiniums are intensely blue as well.

Not only is blue recessive but blue flowers seem less plentiful than others. Spring brings heavenly small ones. There is a rock plant, *Lithospermum diffusum*, aptly named 'Heavenly blue'. There are also scillas, chionodoxa, grape hyacinths, hyacinths and various irises, but most of these are tints or tones rather than primary blue. There is a saying that blue flowers only show to advantage at mid-summer, but this cannot be true, for large expanses of blue in spring are common enough and are quite breath-taking. One has only to think of a bluebell wood.

Summer
The flowers were chosen to make a complementary design in soft tints and tones of blue and peach. White was used chiefly because the design is extremely seasonal and the philadelphus is so summery, but also because the Spode 'Italian' bowl includes white. The flowers are delphiniums, campanulas, Geranium ibericum (border geranium) apricot lilies, honeysuckle and philadelphus. Floral foam provides stem support. (Arranger Pauline Mann)

Summer

Cornflowers are a wonderful primary blue. The spray carnations give a marked contrast of colour, though blue and yellow-cream are not strictly opposites. Lime green is a great unifier of colours, and the Alchemilla mollis does this admirably. The textural effect is rather busy in this freestyle design, but the clear glass container which shows the stems provides a necessary smoothness and a feeling of calm. There are no mechanics.
(Arranger Pauline Mann)

Summer
Delphiniums in tints, tones and shades together with Bristol blue glass against a neutral background. The Alchemilla mollis, grapes and apple give a lively colour contrast. Lime green is one of the most luminous of colours. The echeverias provide a variation of shape and texture. This kind of 'still life' grouping makes a few flowers go a long way. (Arranger Pauline Mann)

3
The Secondary Colours

The secondary pigment colours are the offspring of the primaries. When red and yellow are combined, orange is the result; blue and red make violet; and yellow and blue produce green. When the primary and secondary colours are put together, there are still only six *hues*, but there are hundreds of tints, tones and shades. In fact, the selection of available colours is endless. In terms of flower arranging, the secondary colours are every bit as interesting and important as the primaries.

Orange

Characteristics

Orange is an advancing colour. This means that it is most noticeable when seen and measured against others. Orange has warmth and vitality, and is the colour of fires and sunsets. As well as having physical heat associations, orange symbolizes boldness and brashness. It is often coupled with black and this combination is associated with the Ancient Egyptian period and with Art Deco.

It is sometimes hard to name a colour when viewed on its own. Only when there are several hues in juxtaposition can they be correctly identified. It can also be extremely difficult to remember a colour accurately, particularly when you are trying to match an off-beat tone. Orange is one such elusive colour, and you may find that a true orange only reveals itself when set beside a red or red-orange.

The colour must originally have been named after the fruit. The first mention of oranges in England is during the reign of Queen Elizabeth I, when it is noted that she admired some orange trees belonging to Sir Francis Carew at Beddington, Surrey, in 1591. The sweet orange is said to have come from China, spreading via northern India and south-west Asia into Europe by the ninth century, and reaching Africa and Spain later. Louis XIV of France had a fine orangery built at Versailles in 1685, and it soon became fashionable for the great country houses to follow suit. The trees, planted in tubs, lined garden paths during the summer but were housed in the orangeries in the winter months. Many fine buildings of orangeries can be seen today in gardens open to the public.

Flowers

There is an abundance of orange flowers, beginning in spring with the early *Chaenomeles speciosa* 'Fascination', with its orange blossoms on the bare branches. Dozens of tulips follow. A browse through a good bulb catalogue will show a selection of orange varieties that will bloom between February and late May. One of the flowers that is intensely orange is the biennial Siberian wallflower, *Cheiranthus allionii*. Another is the common marigold, *Calendula officinalis*, which seeds itself, making an orange carpet on a waste place if left alone.

Orange roses are plentiful in all the tints, tones and shades. Lilies are also a striking orange. The *Alstroemeria aurantiaca* 'Moerheim's Orange' is hardier and more orange than the ligtu hybrids. There are several hybrid lilies including relations of the old tiger lily. 'Enchantment' can be seen everywhere and bought cheaply on market stalls; once a luxury, it is now commonplace. Gladioli, dahlias and zinnias all have some zinging colours until cut down by the frosts when the chrysanthemums, far less aggressive in tone, will give orange blooms of different shapes and sizes.

One of the most striking orange flowers is the gerbera. This has such a compulsive, circular shape and an intense, near-fluorescent hue. Natives of South Africa, gerberas are now grown by many countries that export flowers, particularly Holland, and are available all the year round. I admire their sang-froid: a daisy-flower always appears unruffled but the colour makes them conspicuously alien. Indeed, they tend to look out of place arranged with English herbaceous flowers, and are best left on their own in an array of brilliant colour.

Foliage

If seasons have colours, then orange belongs to the autumn. The first sign of its approach is when the berries of the rowan (*Sorbus aucuparia*) start to turn colour. This varies slightly according to the weather, but often the berries begin their colour change in July – a rather saddening early herald of 'the fall'. Not all sorbus have orange berries; many have red fruits. *Sorbus hupehensis* has green berries that eventually change to white tinged with pink, and *Sorbus hupehensis* 'Pink Form' has pink berries. The two latter trees keep their fruits until Christmas, as do those rowans with yellow berries. The birds wait greedily for both orange and red kinds to ripen and, as soon as they do, they demolish them very quickly. The diarist John Evelyn (1620–1706) noted that the birds who fed on the berries became intoxicated with them. Interestingly, the sorbus, or rowan, is planted near to houses or garden gates in some parts of the country to keep the witches away. This is certainly a custom still practised in remote parts of Yorkshire.

The wild arum, known as 'lords-and-ladies', raises its green-berried stalk during August and turns a brilliant orange slowly, berry by berry. The cultivated *Arum italicum* 'Pictum' behaves in exactly the same way.

When the trees change colour, every possible tint, tone and shade of yellow and orange unite for a few fleeting weeks, turning the hedges and woods into a blaze of fire. The trees that show their colours most flamboyantly are the acers, crataegus (thorns), malus (crabs), certain prunus (cherries) and various sorbus. Any experienced nurseryman will recommend garden trees that give good autumn colour.

Mock orange (*philadelphus*) is a commonly grown summer-flowering shrub with highly scented white flowers. There are many varieties to choose from. Because of the perfume it is a most romantic shrub, which should be visited in the darkness of a summer's night, when its scent is overpowering. Like all trees and shrubs that flower after the leaves appear it needs defoliating or the foliage hides the blossoms, detracting from their fragility. Growing, with leaves obliterating flowers, these are trees to be smelt rather than looked at.

Summer
A vibrant arrangement of complementary colours. Pure hues of orange lilies and blue delphiniums are set against a bright checked tablecloth and blue Bristol glass.
(Arranger Daphne Vagg)

High summer

These colours are slightly autumnal. The apricots and nectarines are so in harmony with the alstroemeria and 'Festival' lilies that it would be a shame not to put them near to each other! The green Wedgwood stand and plate add contrast to the group, which also contains Alchemilla mollis and the seed heads of Heuchera sanguinea *'Greenfinch'. There is floral foam in a tin on the stand.*
(Arranger Pauline Mann)

Green

Characteristics

Green, nature's colour, signifies life. It is the colour of the earth's trees and plants that support the entire animal life of the world. We are completely dependent on the oxygen manufactured in the green leaves by the process of photosynthesis. Without green, there is no human life. Green is a cool colour. It is opposite red on the colour wheel, and like blue it induces peace and relaxation. Green is symbolically the colour of envy, of innocence and of ignorance.

Foliage

Flower arrangers prize foliage beyond rubies. They crave the demonstrator's left-overs for cuttings and resist throwing away the smallest piece. How often is heard the comment, 'It is so lovely with the foliage only that I feel I don't want to use the flowers.' Nowadays the vogue is for more space within floral designs, and flowers are seldom cheek to cheek; instead, blooms are separated or framed instead by well-chosen foliage, which is just as important as the flowers.

There cannot be more variations amongst the greens than other colours, for the permutations are limitless for every hue, but there does seem to be an endless selection, ranging between yellow-green and blue-green, as well as a third excursion into silver-green. There can be nothing more breathtakingly beautiful than the lime-green haze of *Salix babylonica* in early spring. If only trees retained their tender freshness and did not – like every other living thing – mature, coarsen and darken, losing their bright youthfulness. By the beginning of July the trees, full and heavy with middle-age, are welcome shade from the hot sun, but they do make sky-hiding umbrellas on cloudy days. Nevertheless, adolescent or mature leaves continue to photosynthesize, a process that takes place only in the green portion of the leaf, not in the white, cream or yellow variegated parts.

This is why variegated specimens are less robust, grow more slowly and usually cost more.

Evergreens

The first time I heard a lecturer at a horticultural college talk on garden planning I was surprised when he recommended two-thirds of evergreens to one-third deciduous shrubs and trees. My reaction was one of slight indignation, partly, I think, because I visualized rows of *Chamaecyparis lawsoniana* and *Cupressocyparis leylandii*. Since then I have learnt about the fascinating variety of form and colour amongst the conifers, and have also come to appreciate all the evergreens that clothe the garden throughout the year and prevent it from resembling a building site during the winter. No wonder our forefathers venerated evergreens and brought them into the winter solstice celebrations, just as we do at Christmas. Primitive people have always worshipped trees, and tree-cults are to be found everywhere. The most prominent characteristic of Teutonic religion was the sanctity attached to certain trees and groves. The most famous in the northern mythology was the 'world tree', Yggdrasil's ash, which sheltered all living beings. We know how sacred the holm oak was to the Druids and how all evergreens were considered a promise of the continuity of life. The Christian concept of the 'tree of life' seems a natural sequel to earlier pagan tree-worship.

As a child – country born and bred – holly, yew, ivy, box, fir and mistletoe were the only Christmas decorations I cared about. What pleasurable ages it took to twine the ivy round the banisters. Spoilt by the limitless amount of foliage round us in the garden, field and hedge, we were surprised to see paper chains and glittery things decorating the homes of those we felt must be less fortunate than ourselves. Taste has now changed with the increasing scarcity of fresh foliage, and glitter has become the norm. Certainly, it provides a brilliance that is lacking in the rather sombre traditional evergreens.

Summer

Foliage arrangements are immensely popular. They are especially suitable during the summer for they are refreshingly cool looking. The central leaves in the design are those of the Montbretia crocosmiiflora; *there is also* Hedera helix *'Goldheart',* Viburnum tinus *'Variegata',* Euonymus japonicus *'Ovatus Aureus', leaves of* Helleborus foetidus,

Chamaecyparis pisifera, *the fern 'Polystichum setiferum' 'Divisilobum', hostas 'Honeybells' and 'Frances Williams' and the still green seeds of the* Arum italicum *'Pictum'. All arranged in floral foam in a flat green Wedgwood dish.*
(*Arranger Pauline Mann*)

Flowers

Green flowers have a sophistication that belies the naturalness of their colour, and they are much liked by flower arrangers. Many white flowers have a green tinge or green flecks, feathering, edging, stripes and throats. There are lime-green tree flowers – for example, those of the Norway maple, lime and wych elm. *Helleborus corsicus*, H. *foetidus* and H. *viridis* are green, and H. *niger* turns green in the fruiting stage. *Alchemilla mollis* and many of the euphorbias are green too. Then there are the annuals: *Nicotiana* 'Really Green', *Zinnia* 'Envy' and *Amaranthus* 'Viridis'.

Winter
Even when the green of Helleborus foetidus is a tint and the red H. atrorubens a shade, they are still complementary colours. There is a pinholder in the basket the little cherubs are carrying.
(Arranger Pauline Mann)

Anemones and gypsophila
(Arranger Janet Hayton)

36

Purple

Characteristics

Purple is described as a shade varying between crimson and violet. It is a colour that symbolizes panoply and power, and is associated with royalty, the Church and Imperial Rome. It is a rich, uncompromising, cruel colour and yet one of the most beautiful and varied. It is also the colour associated with waiting and penitence. The Church's year has two seasons in which purple is used. Both of these lead up to the two most important festivals in our calendar: Advent is the lead up to Christmas, and Lent prepares us for Easter. There is another sort of waiting, too. In the early morning at dawn and at dusk, the sky is often tinged with deep purple preparing us for either day or night.

Purple became a status symbol in the past because it was made from a rare dye. The shellfish named *Purpura* yielded the celebrated Tyrian dye and was probably the first dye to be permanently fixed on wool or linen. Purpura was also present in other molluscs, and when spread on the cloth it produced a purple-red colour. The amount of dye contained in each shellfish was so small, and the task of extraction so laborious, that very few people could afford the price of purple garments. In heraldry, purple, or purpure, is represented on the metal shields of knights by diagonal lines drawn from sinister to dexter (left to right), so brass rubbers can work out the exact colours used.

Flowers

At the dawn of each year, we look eagerly for signs of spring. Violet winter-flowering pansies that have struggled to keep going through the winter heave a sigh of relief when the warmer weather approaches. The pale purple crocuses open up to the spring sunshine and fill us with joy. In the mossy crannies, on the banks or in the hedgerows, the shy violet peeps its head out to test the weather, and then, deciding it is getting warmer, flowers on through the spring, the flowers getting bigger and bigger as it gains confidence. Aubretia hurls itself over walls and rock gardens in all hues of lilac, mauve, lavender and magenta. The reliable tiny *Primula juliae* 'Wanda' turns its head skywards and keeps on flowering.

If we take out our paint box and add red to our original purple we get magenta. Its colour, a reddish-purple solution called fuchsin, was named after Leonard Fuchs, the German botanist who lived from 1501–66, and was discovered about the time of the Battle of Magenta in Northern Italy in 1859. As well as being an old and well-known dye stuff, magenta was one of the first to be produced synthetically. Synthetic magenta or rosaniline is the most vibrant of the purple hues and was loved by the Victorians, who wore it frilled and flounced in the form of silks, wools and crushed velvet. They covered their walls, curtained their windows and buttoned their spoon-back *chaise longues* with the colour. It is not surprising they suffered from headaches – the colour is very overpowering.

Today, fuchsias adorn our greenhouses and droop from our hanging baskets in the summer, taking their name from the original fuchsin dye. They grow wild in Cornwall and are one of our most-loved plants.

What, however, is true purple? The intense – almost cyclamen – colour of the Church dignitaries' robes is at one end of the scale. 'Born in the purple' refers to rank, whilst promotion to the purple means being elevated to the position of cardinal in the Roman Catholic Church. If the Church's purple is on the red side, think of the variations between the purple clematis and the smooth shiny skin colour of the aubergine and the bloom on the deep purple plums on the market stalls. Think of the shiny purple blue-black grapes hanging in clusters from the vine. If we add a little more red and a tinge of white to our palette we can see a whole valley covered in the pale mauve blossom of rhododendrons. Adding a little more white to the colour, we see climbing wisteria, phlox, stocks and many more tiny wild flowers.

Finally, moving on to autumn, we must add just a little more blue and red again from the paint box to discover Michaelmas daisies, aster and ling. The mountains and heathlands are indeed purple at this rich time of year with the heather in full bloom. Purple and gold of autumn is upon us again, and the violet shine on the breast of the hen pheasant catches the sun.

Spring
This simple arrangement of Anemone coronaria in a bowl makes a
colourful picture on a dull cold day. Notice how much of the effectiveness of
the arrangement depends on the varying sizes of the flower heads.
(Arranger Pauline Mann)

4
Preparing Plant Material

General Tips

Time is well spent in conditioning plant material. To a flower arranger, conditioning means preparing the flowers and foliage after cutting them from the garden or collecting them from the florist, before arranging. The preparation involves treating the various stem types in the correct way, and sometimes removing leaves and thinning out branches before finally putting the material into water for a long drink, preferably for 12 hours, especially if the flowers are to be arranged in floral foam. The shortest time for conditioning – and this would be a rushed job – is two hours, and then the flowers should be put into a vase full of water.

The most important factor to remember – and this applies to all cut plant material – is that a dried stem end cannot take up water properly. This is why the advice to take a bucket of water into the garden when you cut is not as far-fetched as it first sounds: it is a counsel of perfection. If things are put straight into water when cut there is no time for the stem ends to seal over. Every flower has a life span and it will live out that time if it is treated properly.

There are special substances manufactured today that claim to lengthen the life of cut flowers; these may be purchased from the florist. There are also some homely, cheap remedies that can be added to the water, such as an aspirin, a copper coin, a spoonful of sugar, or a drop of household bleach (this is especially successful for carnations). None of these will make the slightest difference if the stem ends are dry, or if there is an airlock in the flower's stem.

Here are some other useful tips:

- Remove leaves that would be under water in the conditioning bucket.
- Tepid water moves up the stems faster than cold water.
- Put flowers in cold water in a dark place if you want to retard them.
- Put flowers in warm water and in a light (not sunlit) place when you want to advance them.

Routine treatments

Woody stems: these are hard-stemmed materials such as tree and shrub branches. Groom the foliage, taking off anything damaged or unwanted. Scrape the bark from the bottom 5cm (2in.) of stem and split it, thus opening up the water intake area. Put into deep water. When you arrange the foliage, cut off the split portion of stem at a slant.

Hard stems: large chrysanthemums and roses come into this category. Remove some of the flowers' foliage, leaving enough to give them character. De-thorn roses. Split the hard stems upwards at the ends for 2.5cm (1in.). Put sprays into tepid water, unless you wish to slow down their opening, in which case use cold water.

Hollow stems: lupins and delphiniums have these stems and require careful conditioning. Turn the flowers upside-down, and with a small spouted watering-can fill the stems before plugging them with a small piece of tissue, cotton-wool or floral foam. Stand them in deep water, after removing the lower leaves.

Milky stems: euphorbias and poppies, for example, exude a milky substance, which is a latex. To prevent this leaking out, the stem ends have to be burnt; a candle or gas

'Trimming a branch'

flame will do the job. Then put them into deep water. If the stems have to be shortened for the arrangement, re-burn them.

Soft stems: this is the kind of stem found on bulbous flowers. All that can be done is to remove the white pithy parts, cutting them off under water. Also under water, re-cut the stem ends if they are dry before conditioning. Bulbs are often sold straight from boxes, so the stem ends have dried completely. Tulips may be wrapped in newspaper before being stood in water, and their flowers develop better if the lower leaves are removed. Avoid split stem ends with all bulbs. They are quite happy in 5cm (2in.) of water in a pinholder.

Immature foliage: all new growth is difficult to condition. When it has to be used defoliate to a certain extent so that no stem is over-loaded with leaves.

Mature foliage: this can be put under water for a few hours, but no longer than overnight. Large, mature single leaves are excellent subjects for the immersion treatment, and can be made to last for weeks if they have their stems re-cut and are then re-soaked, under water, for an hour or so. Fatsia, bergenia, ivy and arum, both the wild arum and the *Arum italicum* 'Pictum', and all hostas respond to being refreshed from time to time.

Grey foliage: this should never be submerged as it will lose its greyness if it goes under water.

Burning stem ends

There are many arrangers who burn all stem ends – other than those of bulbs – as a matter of course, and would not dream of not doing so. It sounds a drastic procedure, destructive rather than beneficial, but the reasons for doing so are:
- the cells subjected to burning are destroyed. This means that the micro-organisms that produce slime, which block the xylem (the part of a plant's vascular tissue that transports water) and foul up the water, are put out of action
- the dead stem ends cannot leak the flowers' nutrients into the water and foul it
- the dead cells cannot form a callus, which would seal the stem end and prevents the uptake of water

- excessive heat expands the air in the stems and helps to get rid of any airlock that may have formed after the flowers were cut (this is the second most common reason for flowers wilting).

Water treatment

1. Begin by cutting off about 5cm (2in.) of stem ends under water. Match the first aid to the type of flower, e.g., soft petals can be damaged if they are left floating in water too for too long, but bracts will come to no harm.
2. Immediately stand the flower in deep tepid water and leave for two hours.
3. Re-cut as above and leave the flower floating in tepid water for an hour or two.
4. If there is foliage attached to the flower remove most of it, re-cut the stem and leave it to float.

Boiling water treatment is nearly always successful for reviving wilting plants. I have known it fail only when the plant material has been so long without water that the cell structure has collapsed.

To do this, re-cut the stem and cover the head of the flower with a soft cloth or tissue paper before standing in 2.5cm (1in.) of boiling water (this is especially recommended for florists' roses). Leave in water until it cools.

How to avoid wilting
- don't put flowers too near a radiator
- make sure the room temperature is not too high
- keep flowers out of direct sunlight
- keep flowers out of draughts
- top up container water daily
- mist-spray flowers and leaves with water to maintain a moist atmosphere

Flowers needing special conditioning

Alliums or any member of the onion family: do not use warm water or the oniony smell will be more pronounced.

Berries: spray with hair lacquer or clear varnish to help to prevent them from shrivelling. Some arrangers condition them in a mixture of sugar and water first.

Bulrushes and reed-mace: spray with hair lacquer or clear varnish to stop them from blowing. Gather them well before they are ripe.

Clematis: defoliate and condition the leaves separately. Float the flowers for an hour. They are composed of petal-like sepals and – in some species – petal-like stamens.

Euphorbias: all must have their stem ends burnt.

Geraniums: choose inflorescences with plenty of buds as well as open flowers. Spray the backs of the flowers carefully with clear varnish to prevent the petals drooping.

Gerberas: these flowers are not lovers of floral foam and can be temperamental. The best method is to fill a deep bucket with water and either cover it with a cap of 2.5cm (1in.) wire netting or cut holes in a box lid through which the flower stems may be slotted. Leave the flower heads resting on the wire or cardboard for support. Adding fizzy lemonade to the water is also recommended.

Hellebores: there are many species and all last longer if cut after their seed-pods have ripened. *Helleborus niger* is one of the hardest to condition, but they all respond to having the surface skin of the stems slit with a pin. Start the slit just under the flower head – or cluster – and draw the pin down to the stem end. Then submerge the flower and stem for an hour. Hellebores do not like floral foam and should be arranged in deep water. If they flag, re-cut the stems and float for a while.

Hydrangeas: another of the inflorescences composed of coloured bracts. They need constant humidity, so spray frequently. Split the stem ends and condition by floating, having first taken off any leaves.

Lilies: although it is a shame to take away a flower's character in any way, it is sometimes necessary to cut off the anthers of lilies as the pollen can ruin clothes and stain the petals. It does depend upon the occasion, but for a wedding it is advisable. The arum lily is different. All lilies need straightforward conditioning, and they last well.

Molucella laevis: defoliate.

Violets: need high humidity, so spray frequently or float.

Water lilies: pour cooling melted wax (such as candle wax) into the flowers' centres to stop them from closing.

Zinnias: these flowers have weak stems so push a stub wire through the flower head into the stem of each to prevent them from bending.

Forcing branches

It is enormously pleasurable to bring branches of flowering shrubs or trees early in the year into a living room and watch them respond to the warmth. Obviously, the nearer the branches are to their natural flowering or leafing time, the quicker they will show colour, but they may be brought inside at any time as long as their buds show. It is a great joy to watch forsythia open its canary-yellow blossoms and to see ribes – flowering currant – open the palest of pink blooms, for this well-known shrub's flowers are almost white when they are forced. *Chaenomeles*, too, has lighter flowers when forced. Chestnuts, maples, the corkscrew willow and most deciduous trees can give weeks of interest indoors. They will benefit from deep water that should be changed weekly and a spray every few days, especially if the room is hot and the air dry. Condition stem ends as advised for 'woody' (see p.00).

Retarding flowers

Sometimes, when flowers are needed for a special occasion, it is disappointing if they are over before the event. Gladioli and peonies can be retarded. Cut them a week in advance, with the buds showing a small amount of colour. Put them in a cool, dark place, out of water, until two days before they are wanted. Then cut 5cm (2in.) off the stem ends under water, plunge into deep, warm water and stand in a good light – not full sunlight – for 48 hours.

Simple retarding can be done by placing tighter buds in cold water in a dark place. Roses will stay in bud quite satisfactorily when treated this way. Once a flower is fully open there is not much that can be done to prevent it from 'blowing', though it might be worth while giving the back a gentle spray with a clear varnish.

It is possible, however, to prevent roses from opening wide. Lightly beat up an egg white and with a soft paint

brush touch the inside of the outer petals with the white.
Tie the flower head carefully with wool until the egg white
has set. When the wool is taken off the petals will unfold no
further. Buds may have wool tied around them until they
have been arranged. At the last minute take off the wool
and the roses will open slowly.

Summer
*A bowl of flowers that merges with the surroundings. 'New Dawn' roses of
the softest possible pink, 'Doris' pinks and Polygonum affine of slightly
stronger hue mixed with grey foliage. The effect is restful and very sweet
smelling. The bowl stands on a carved wooden plinth. Mechanics –
pinholder.*
(Arranger Pauline Mann)

5
Preserving Plant Material

Nowadays there are few households without plant material in some form or other. The number of garden centres increases all the time and can only be in response to a demand. The conservatory, so loved by the Victorians, is back in fashion for the fortunate who have both space and money to erect one, and one constantly sees areas in living rooms where growing plants are grouped to give a 'green bower' effect. Arrangers still enjoy preserving flowers, however, and use dried or glycerined items throughout the year and not just during the winter.

Methods of preservation have improved over the last decade, and the acceptance of the use of paints and sprays in much competitive work has increased the range of colour and widened the field for the use of preserved material.

There are those who have a genuine love for dried flowers and leaves, even preferring them to fresh arrangements. It is the muted and subtle colouring that appeals to people – obviously no paints or sprays are needed for them. These captive flowers, suspended in time, have another attribute: they can remind us of past events – the pressed picture made from flowers gathered on a special holiday, or the dome of desiccant-dried flowers that formed the wedding bouquet.

The ways of preserving are:

- pressing
- glycerining
- drying in desiccant
- air and heat drying
- skeletonizing

Dried material may be bleached and, if you wish, everything or anything can be touched up with water paint or spray; some glycerined materials will even absorb dye with the glycerine.

Here are some uses for the preserved plant material:

pressed pictures

3-D pictures, glazed, in box frames

spice posies or trees

topiary trees

dried posies

garlands

swags and collages

book markers, especially for Church festivals and weddings

phantom bouquets, the Victorians' name for a skeletonized arrangement

table mats and door plates – these need to be heat sealed

keyrings

cards and calendars

decorated boxes

samplers

dome arrangements

Whatever the method of preservation there are some basic points to remember that are applicable to all techniques:

1. Don't waste time preserving the imperfect; groom the plant material thoroughly and discard all damaged leaves and flowers.
2. Pick all material for pressing or drying when it is quite dry.
3. Always gather a variety of sizes and shapes from bud to open flower, and different sized leaves. This applies especially to articles to be pressed when every aspect of a flower is needed – profile, back and face.
4. Don't overcrowd the blotting paper when pressing, the jar or bucket when glycerining or bleaching, or the box when using a desiccant.
5. Keep an eye on the progress of everything apart from the items in the press, which can come to no harm.

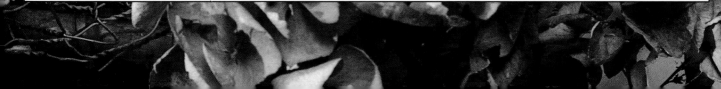

Late autumn or winter

Because dried flowers are always subdued in colour it is hard to realize how many hues are contained in the basket. Market stalls have greatly increased their supplies of flowers for drying over the last few years. These cost far less than those already dried and bunched in craft shops or similar places. Quantity is important when using dried materials; they should give a feeling of abundance. The round basket is packed full and there is no foliage. A double layer of 2.5cm (1in.) wire-netting is fitted into the entire round of the basket to hold the stems firmly.
(Arranger Pauline Mann)

Air drying

Immortelles

The 'immortelles' are the flowers that dry naturally and, when grouped together, produce a considerable range of colour. They are easy to grow in the garden but may be bought from markets and good florists' shops from early July onwards. The picture on page 48 shows a selection of these. Immortelles or everlastings dry crisply and feel straw-like – all the drier has to do is to strip off the leaves, tie them in small bundles and hang them upside-down in an airy place. The colour retention is best when this is done in a dim light; sunlight will obviously fade them eventually.

Helichrysum bracteatum is the most familiar; these have to be given false stems *before* they are dried. Cut off the flower's natural stem, then simply push a wire of 0.7mm (22 gauge) into the flower's centre either from above or underneath; if you are threading from above, you can make a hook, although this is not vital as the wire rusts into the flower and so should not fall off. *Helichrysum bracteatum* comes in rosy colours, creamy yellow and various orange shades. They need not be hung up and will dry standing on

their new wire stems in jars in a warm, airy place. Their tiny buds should be cut off from the plants too, and spread out in a shallow box. They will expand as they dry and make charming little flowers that can be used for many decorations.

Helipterum manglesii and *Helipterum roseum* (or *Acroclinium roseum*) are of various shades of pink. Their stems, although minute in diameter, are wiry enough to support the almost weightless flowers, which are far more attractive when bunched together rather than arranged singly; tape the stems with seven or so flowers forming a cluster. *Xeranthemum annum*, another daisy-like bloom, has mauve, pinky-mauve and white flowers and quite strong, straight stems. *Limonium sinuatum* dries without trouble when hung. It has bright flowers of purple, yellow, white cream, pink and two shades of blue.

All the above immortelles are annuals. A perennial that dries in like manner to the annuals is anaphalis, with its small clusters of white daisy flowers. There are several species with similar inflorescences. If the fluffy centres are removed after the flowers have dried you are left with neat flat daisies with green-brown middles – very pretty indeed.

Other perennials that dry well are the achilleas, *Physalis alkekengi* and *P. franchetii*, known as Chinese lanterns, and the astrantias. But there are plenty of plants whose successful drying and good colour retention depends upon your skill. Most importantly, they must be cut at the correct stage of development. This group contains larkspur, delphiniums, echinops and eryngium.

The largest proportion of dried material comes in the shape of grasses and seedheads. These should be left on the plant to dry, but don't leave them too long in case they are spoilt by the weather.

Hydrangeas

Gather the heads in early autumn when they are just beginning to turn colour and feel slightly crisp. Defoliate and place near a boiler or radiator or slot behind a storage heater for 24 hours. This is the quick method of drying and will not fail unless the heat is insufficient or the flower-heads are not mature enough. A slower way of drying is to stand the defoliated blooms in 5cm (2in.) of water. Leave them until they are dry but do not add any more water.

Winter
A blue background enhances the star-like heads of dried hogweed. The glass container and perspex base helps to capture this ethereal quality. The shiny honesty pennies have been placed in balls of dry foam to give the appearance of round flowers.
(Arranger Pauline Mann)

Project: Making a topiary tree

The topiary tree is made from dried hydrangeas. Use a small amount of car-body spray paint to liven up the colour and disperse painted artificial fruits amongst the flower heads.

Set a dowelling rod in concrete in the flower pot. Top the rod with a ball of dry floral foam and strengthen it with a covering of 2.5cm (1in.) wire netting, fastened by reel wire through holes which you have drilled in the dowelling rod.

Hide the flower pot in a basket and cover the concrete with reindeer moss and one hydrangea head. Finally, bind the rod with some attractive velvet ribbon.

You may find that some of the hydrangeas need a false stem to lengthen them. In this case, place a piece of stubwire alongside the flower stem as shown in the drawing. Then loop a fine wire between the flowers and wind it round the stubwire and the stem. Tape the wires together as shown in the illustration for strength and stability.

The finished tree shown here was about 1 metre (3ft) high.

Topiary Tree
The topiary tree is made from dried greeny-blue
hydrangeas. A discreet amount of car-body spray was
used on some of the flower heads to enliven the colours a
little and painted artificial fruits are dispersed amongst
them.
(Arranger Pauline Mann)

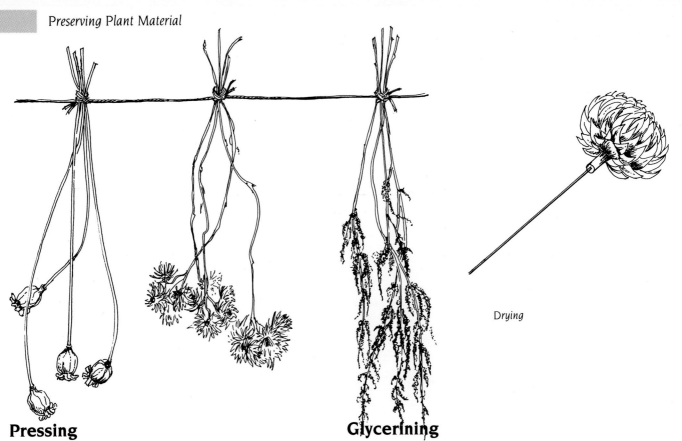

Drying

Pressing

This is a simple means of preserving plant material. It is inexpensive as no special equipment is necessary apart from some sheets of blotting paper and a heavy book. A flower press is pleasant to have but isn't essential; an old telephone directory will do the duty of a press, though it must be evenly weighted to give satisfactory results. The advantage of the press is that the pressure is easily adjustable and uniform. However, whether a press or a book is used, the longer the flowers and leaves are left, the better they will retain their colour. Six months is not too long, and three to four weeks is the absolute minimum.

Here are some useful tips for pressing

- don't be afraid to take bulkier subjects apart for pressing – they can be reassembled later
- succulents are not suitable for pressing
- when making a picture a third dimension can be hinted at by overlapping some of the material
- be sure the glass presses tightly against the flowers in the finished picture; this not only keeps them flat but excludes the air and so helps them to retain their colour

Glycerining

During this operation a diluted glycerine solution takes the place of water in the plant material, making it pliable, glossy and long-lasting.

The usual mixing proportion is one part glycerine to two parts water. Put the glycerine into a vessel large enough to hold the plant material to be treated. Pour boiling water on to the glycerine and stir well. Woody-stemmed items should have the bark scraped off for 5cm (2in.) and the stems split. They can then go straight into the hot solution; for other stem types allow the mixture to cool first. It is possible to use too much glycerine; when this happens, the leaves will begin to exude beads of moisture. Removing the material before all of it has turned brown, as detailed above, prevents over-glycerining. A depth of 5cm (2in.) is enough for the stems to stand in, but top this up when necessary.

Flowers will not take up glycerine, but seedheads, bracts and most foliages will. The resulting colours vary from pale cream through to dark brown. The thickness of different leaves, the stage of their development, the time of year and the temperature of the room where they are being treated have an effect on the speed at which the material takes up the mixture. A warm, not hot, atmosphere is best. Light also affects the results: paler browns are produced by preserving in a good light – though never in direct sunshine

– whilst dark corners will produce darker leaves. However, certain plants can be relied upon always to turn out the same, for example, *Molucella laevis*, known as 'bells of Ireland' and greatly valued by all arrangers, responds well to the process by giving us beautiful cream bracts. Other plants that turn cream are: *Danae racemosa*; *Ruscus aculeatus*; and R. *hypoglossum*; *Aspidistra elatior*; *Choisya ternata*; *Fatshedera lizei*; and *Polygonatum* x *hybridum* – Solomon's seal.

Very large leaves such as those of *Fatsia japonica* need to be covered with the glycerine solution in a shallow dish.

Recently it has become the vogue to take the material out of the solution as soon as the centre of the leaves goes brown. The leaves, or branches, are then tied and hung upside-down until the rest turns colour. This is especially successful with ruscus and moluccella, which complete the process quite fast. With some things the last few leaves turn colour rather slowly, but by removing them from the glycerine earlier more space is made for a quicker turnover of plant material.

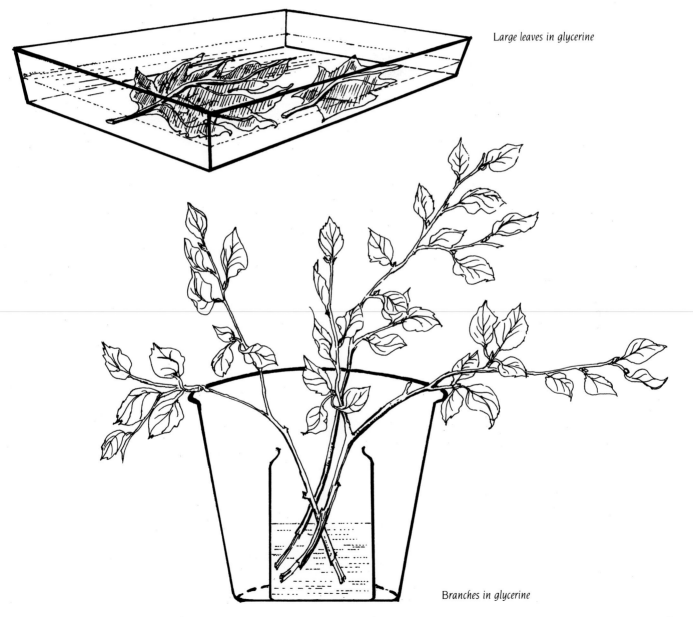

Large leaves in glycerine

Branches in glycerine

Drying with desiccants

This is a fascinating occupation requiring patience and considerable care. The rewards – when all goes well – are flowers that retain their natural colour and form. You will be able to admire all kinds of spring and summer flowers, under protective glass, in winter time. Yet, because these are preserved flowers, there is none of the feeling of unsuitability that flowers out of season provoke. Once dried, these fragile things *must* be kept free from humidity or they will collapse. An arrangement under a dome or in a glazed box frame is a very attractive feature in a room.

Borax, alum, biological washing powder and clean river sand

All these may be used as desiccants. Borax and alum are cheaper than silica gel and are used by many people with success. The washing powder succeeds for some and river sand is quite reliable but very slow.

Silica gel

Silica gel rarely fails; if it does, however, it is the drier's fault! It can be purchased from a chemist, in which case it may need further refinement, or from a firm specializing in flower arranging aids, in which case it will be of the correct texture. The specially-prepared silica gel comes slightly tinted and when the colour disappears it is time to reactivate it; this usually needs doing between each batch of flowers. Instructions will come with the gel, so follow them carefully and remember to remove all the stems, replacing them with fine wire *before* putting the flowers into desiccant. Flowers dried this way must be kept in an air-tight container at all times. Fleshy leaves and flowers are not suitable for this method of preservation. Reactivate the gel by heating it according to the supplier's instruc-

tions – it is usually about 30 minutes at a temperature of 121°C (250°F), and it will need a stir during this time. Be sure to let it cool before using it again.

When using silica gel

you will need:

- an air-tight box
- silica gel
- tweezers
- prepared flowers
- a small paint brush

Method

Pour a 2.5cm (1 in.) layer of desiccant into the box. Space out the plant material on to the desiccant, double flowers facing upwards and single flowers facing downwards. Trickle the desiccant around and into the flowers, shaking the box gently so the crystals penetrate all the crevices. Cover the flowers completely to a depth of at least 2.5cm (1 in.).

Close the box tightly and tape it if necessary. Thin petals, for example primroses, will take only 24 hours, but double flowers and those with thicker petals will take longer – 36 to 48 hours, although it is impossible to be precise when so much depends on the condition of the flowers, the strength of the gel, etc. The material will not be harmed if you examine it after 24 hours and have to replace it in the gel. When the flowers are papery, brush off the crystals and immediately put the flowers into an air-tight box until you are ready to assemble them under glass.

You will need the wire stems if the flowers are to be arranged under a dome, but cut off the wires if they are to be stuck to a background under glass in a box frame.

Summer
Drying flowers in silica gel is very exciting and rewarding – if time consuming! The gel needs to be reactivated (dried out) between every batch and boxes mustn't be overcrowded. Thin petals and simple flowers are the easiest and quickest to dry. The summer wreath contains philadelphus, pansies, blue border geraniums, Nazomi roses, alchemilla, primroses and feverfew – all tightly sealed into a box frame.
(Arranger Pauline Mann)

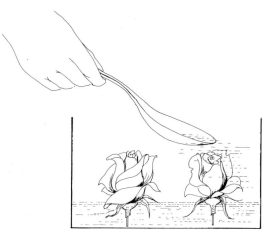

Skeletonizing

It was Victorian young ladies with time on their hands who skeletonized leaves and seedheads and made them into 'phantom bouquets'. We are able to buy bundles of skeletonized magnolia leaves, all faultlessly treated, from the florist or flower club stall, but if you would like to try to do some for yourself, the methods are listed below. Always remember that a leaf must be mature before it can be skeletonized, and whatever else, it needs to be thick.

It is worth while having a forage under holly trees, magnolias and rhododendrons to see if nature has done any skeletonizing for you, or there may be some that are half done that you could finish off. *Nicandra physalides* (shoo-fly plant), *Molucella laevis* bracts and the orange balloons of *Physalis alkekengi and* P. *franchetii* often skeletonize themselves. Any leaves found in the garden may need a short spell in a bleach solution before being thoroughly rinsed, dried and flattened between blotting paper.

Method 1

When you have chosen suitable leaves, put them into a bucket of rain water and leave them for some weeks – six to twelve. By this time the epidermis will be spongy enough to be removed by being gently scraped with a knife *or* by being 'pounded' with a tooth brush.

Method 2

Boil the leaves in a strong solution of household soda and water (use an old saucepan). Half a packet of washing powder may be substituted for the soda, in which case boil the leaves for half an hour and allow them to cool before scraping or 'pounding'.

Bleaching

However hard I try and however strong I make the solution, I cannot bleach cones to the creaminess of those done commercially. But many dried materials benefit from a spell immersed in a bucket containing one part of bleach to two of water, or, for obstinate cases, equal parts. The resulting pale colours are such a valuable contrast to all the browns of glycerined foliage, which can look heavy. Bleach will also restore to cleanliness anything soiled by the weather, such as agapanthus seedheads, the indispensable hog-weed spokes and hydrangea bracts. The hydrangeas sometimes skeletonize if they are left in the bleach for too long. But it is amazing how tough plant materials are, for a couple of hours in the bleach apparently does them no harm and often I have left something in for longer. It is essential to rinse everything very thoroughly in cold water to get rid of all traces of the bleach and its smell.

Both bleached and skeletonized plant material can be painted or sprayed.

Skeletonizing a leaf

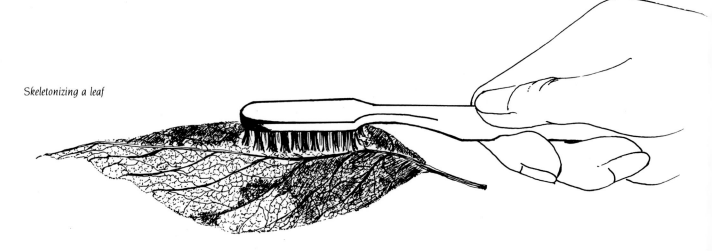

Autumn

By the end of September at the latest hydrangeas feel slightly crisp and this is the time to gather them for drying. The picture shows a medley of blue and blue-green arranged in floral foam in a peacock blue container standing on a piece of a William Morris fabric. Alongside is a Victorian solitaire board. If the hydrangeas are left alone in the floral foam – no further water added – they should gradually dry for winter use. (Arranger Pauline Mann)

6
Containers and Mechanics

One definition of a vase is 'a vessel of greater height than width', so a bowl is probably a vessel of greater width than height. Today, flower arranging containers come in all different styles and materials – anything from a painted tin or saucer to a valuable porcelain or alabaster vessel. The only essential requirement is that the container should hold water or have space for an inner water reservoir. 'Mechanics' is the term that describes all devices for securing the stems of cut plant material.

Mechanics

Stem-holding devices appear to have been thought of in every civilization. The ancient Egyptians made dishes for lotus flowers with a raised bar in the centre under which the flowers' thick stems could be pushed to secure them. The narrow-necked vase used in China held – and still holds – flower stems tightly. Tops with holes in were made for bowls and jars; later there were wire spirals and other wire contraptions that exactly fitted the aperture of the container. Our mothers and grandmothers had glass 'roses' that made each flower stand bolt upright equidistant from its neighbour. But I am sure people always improvised, and perhaps they discovered the 'desert island' remedies thousands of years ago: sand, stones, thick cut stems of some other plant packed into the container to support whatever was being arranged; even chopped-up fabric might have been used. Thank goodness we have pinholders, wire netting and plastic foams today.

Floral foam

Oasis and other water-retaining plastic foams have completely revolutionized flower arranging. Like most things that become a boon there is a reverse side: flowers don't last as long in foam as water, and they always look less natural. Yet although designs can give the impression of being too accurate, too precise, floral foams are a godsend in many ways. They allow speedy arranging; garland making becomes simple; and cones, swags, topiary trees and mechanics for other difficult designs are far steadier. Arrangements can also be transported safely. But perhaps the most important attribute of the foams is that we are able to give the plant material a graceful downwards flow. There are no other mechanics that make it possible for every flower or branch to be placed at exactly the height, depth and angle required in a mass arrangement – no wonder some look manipulated!

There are many brands of floral foam, and all sorts of shapes and sizes. Those for dried flowers are usually brown but can sometimes be green, so it is best to ask the florist's advice when buying them. A glance through a flower-arranging magazine will give the names of the various foams and the cheap plastic containers into which certain shapes fit. When you cut the foam use a sharp knife and cut it cleanly. *Remember*:

- It must be taller than the rim of the container.
- Do not oversoak it – 10 minutes is usually long enough but light-weight grades may need less time. If you leave a large block in a washing-up bowl of water, by the time it has sunk to the bottom it will have taken in enough water.
- Whatever the size of an arrangement the foam should not touch the sides of the container. Otherwise the plant material will syphon and also there will be no room for watering.
- All foams should be topped up every day. Make sure there is a finger's space between the foam and the sides of the container so you can feel how dry it is.
- Once soaked, none of the floral foams should be allowed to dry out because they won't take up water again properly. If there is a piece that can be used again, wrap it in cling film or enclose it in a plastic bag.

Floral tape

This is a sticky tape of various widths sold in rolls for the purpose of securing the floral foam to the container. It is available from florists.

Floral adhesive

This is a substance rather like chewing gum and it certainly makes things stick. It is excellent for anchoring a pinholder to its container. Both container and pinholder must be bone dry, however, for it to work properly. To release a pinholder stuck with this substance, just give it a twist.

Floral foam holder

These are like lead pinholders but have fewer pins to secure the floral foam. Not only is the floral foam prevented from slipping but also weight is added to the mechanics when such a holder is used.

The sprog

A sprog is a small green plastic floral foam holder. It is very light and is fixed to the container with a dab of floral adhesive to stop the foam moving in a small arrangement.

Pinholders

The pinholder is Japanese in origin. It is called a *kenzan* or a sword mountain in Japan. A heavy lead pinholder closely inset with brass pins is one of the best types to buy. Never buy a cheap or plastic version; these are useless because they are too light and the pins aren't sharp enough – both crucial factors. A vase containing an arrangement is easily toppled over, and a heavy pinholder in the bottom is an important stabilizer, along with water.

Pinholders are made in several sizes and in various shapes. However, the round ones are the most useful. A good size to own is one between 5cm and 7.5cm (2in. and

A container on a stand. Wire netting secures the floral foam

3in.); when firmly anchored, this will take the weight of enough plant material for an average arrangement. Floral adhesive will bond a pinholder to any smooth, dry surface. If you don't want the container to be seen, find a small tin that is just deep enough to permit the pins to be covered with water.

Well-pinholder

This is a 'built-in' pinholder of considerable weight. When buying one, choose a well with sloping sides that is not too deep.

Wire netting

Plastic-coated wire can be obtained from a florist's shop and is very useful for house-sized designs. The ordinary wire netting from a hardware store is, however, stronger and because of its colour is better for use in the top of a glass vase. It is almost invisible if painted or sprayed silver. Ordinary wire netting is the best means of supporting swags and garlands made in floral foam. The 2.5cm (1in.) mesh is advisable for wedging into vases and for the swags and garlands, but 5cm (2in.) mesh, crumpled up, is the most useful in large bowls.

The base

A mat was originally placed under the container to protect the furniture in the Western world. Chinese vases always

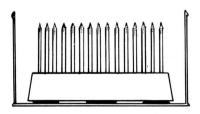

The pinholder must be covered with water

had their own carved stands, and perhaps it is these that inspired the West to be more ambitious about what was placed under the vase. It is a comparatively modern trend to make a feature of the base by covering a cake board with material and finishing it with a circle of braid. Small trays, trivets and pieces of smooth wood are also appropriate as stands. It depends entirely on what you want from your flowers: if they are to be an important feature, the use of a base helps to accentuate them. A base somehow 'presents' flowers. If, on the other hand, you want the flowers to look casual – as though you had just gathered them and slipped them into a vase – then a base may be out of place. It is always sensible to protect furniture, however.

Containers

Small flowers are pretty in jugs, cups, wine glasses and mugs. All kinds of receptacles can be adapted: old sugar basins, baskets and bowls, though not designed as vases, are most attractive. The colour of the container matters a great deal: muted colours are good because they don't detract from the flowers. Grey, soft green, grey-green, brown, fawn, black and earthy colours are excellent. It is easy to see why soft green and grey-green are favoured, for green is present in all flowers, so a greenish container is a natural link with stems and foliage. White, although neutral, may be too advancing and dominant; it is always said that a white container should have some white flowers included in the design to unite the container with the flowers. However, white has been, and still is, popular.

Summer
A dark green modern container with two openings, each supplied with a pinholder. Marguerites of differing lengths are used with gypsophila to soften the outline.
(Arranger Pauline Mann)

Suiting the container to the flowers

Because nearly everything that will hold water can be used as a vase there are a few points to bear in mind when deciding what to select.

- The scale of the container should relate to the size of the flowers or the mass of flowers that will go into it.
- The container's colour should be either neutral or linked by being adjacent to the colour of the flowers. For a modern setting the contrast of a complementary colour is often attractive.
- The style of the container should be in harmony with the manner in which the flowers are arranged and with the ambience of the room.

Wire netting in a tall vase

Patterned containers

It would be absurd to dismiss patterned containers as unsuitable as there are so many beautiful ones around. You can usually see at a glance whether or not a decoration detracts from the flowers. This is an instance when the furnishings of the room have to be considered. There were many periods in history when everything appears to have been patterned, so if a room has a Chinese, rococo or Victorian flavour, a painted vase will be quite at home. There is also much rustic pottery that can be charming when filled with informal bunches. But modern rooms, with their feeling of space, need bold undecorated pots that depend on good lines for their attraction. Over-decoration can spoil good lines.

Urns

There is plenty of evidence that the ancient Egyptians made vessels especially for flowers; they also put plant material including fruit and vegetables into baskets, piling them high for table decorations. The ancient Greeks have always been renowned for their architecture and for perfectly proportioned and shaped urns, water and wine holders. But apart from a few wall paintings showing women placing branches in tall, decorated vases, there is only the thinnest evidence that flowers were arranged in water. In classical times there were expert garland and wreath makers who used either to bind or set foliage and flowers on to creeping fig or vine stems. Both the Greeks and Romans had baskets and cornucopia made of wicker, metal and sometimes stone, but it is impossible to know if they used the metal and stone vessels, with water in them, for flowers. One of the earliest records of arranged flowers is, however, Roman, and is a mosaic of a wicker basket of mixed flowers from the Quintilii Villa on the Appian Way, dating from the second century AD.

Although vases as such were not important to these people, the shape of their vessels has been a continuous source of inspiration to the Western world ever since. Today there are many good replicas manufactured in a variety of materials, including plastic. Urns present no problems with mechanics, but because of their traditional shape they inevitably need a design to match.

It is a truism to say that flowers are happiest in plenty of water, but it is worth noting that deep water, pinholders and wire-netting are cheaper than floral foam and in many cases help the flowers to last longer. Foam is responsible for the over-arranged look, which some people find too precise. Here are four alternative methods suitable for arranging flowers in an urn:

1 Loosely crumple a piece of 2.5cm or 5cm (1in. or 2in.) wire netting – it should be loosely crumpled because if the wire is too solid the stems will not be able to find a way through. Netting on its own works best in the deepest urns.
2 Place a large pinholder into an urn before adding some crumpled wire-netting on top of it, catching some strands of wire on the pinholder to prevent the wire moving about. The pinholder also gives excellent support for the tallest upright stems.
3 Impale the foam on a holder before taping it to the container with floral tape made for the purpose. The holder will give extra base weight, which is always an advantage. The foam *must* stand at least 5cm (2in.) above the rim of any container, otherwise a downward flow of plant material is impossible.
4 When the container is large and foam has to be built up, use a cover of wire-netting to strengthen it and take some of the weight of the stems. Reel wire will fasten the cover of wire netting to the urn's handles. If there are no handles, put a tight band of wire or a thick rubber band around the container – preferably just under its rim – and fix the reel wire to either of these.

The narrow-necked vase

Narrow-necked vases were used by the Chinese as early as AD 960, which is when their flower history was first documented. China, known as the 'flowery kingdom', has always had containers covered with floral decorations. The Chinese put branches of flowering trees or shrubs into the small openings, which held them tightly. Genuine or reproduction Chinese vases look extremely beautiful treated this way. A few churches still have narrow-necked brass altar vases, and sometimes a candlecup is fastened to them.

Jugs

Jugs are satisfying domestic utensils of great character and have become collector's items. They are manufactured in every conceivable material and may be elegant, cottage, or modern – the variety is endless. They make splendid containers, especially for the informal arrangement, perhaps put together in the hand and tied before being placed in the jug. A large jug can contain crumpled wire and a pinholder for mechanics, in which case the flowers would need to be put in one by one.

Spring

Tints and tones of pink with neutral white are in a harmonious setting. Although there is a wide choice of tulips in the florists', there are even more exciting varieties to be grown in one's own garden. This photograph shows lily-flowered 'Marilyn', May-flowering 'Smiling Queen' and 'Kryptos' along with white stocks, gypsophila and the exquisite grey foliage of Sorbus aria 'Lutescens'. A dark green background would have made a more sophisticated setting, but against a patterned background the tulips would loose their delicate marking. Mechanics – a pinholder and crumpled wire-netting.

(Arranger Pauline Mann)

Glass

Glass vases, plain, cut or moulded, were once a part of every household's equipment. It wasn't until the arrival of floral foam that glass fell from grace and it became unfashionable to show the stems of the flowers. Now glass is back in fashion, and containers tend to be simple and chunky, and it is deliciously refreshing to see flower stems encrusted with bubbles. The mechanics have to be simple and invisible; the most satisfactory is a piece of crumpled wire-netting wedged tightly in the opening. The wire can be sprayed or painted silver first to make it even less visible.

A simple aid for glass or modern ceramic containers is the Japanese kubari; this is a forked stick of living – not dried – wood of a suitable thickness. The wood is cut to fit tightly across the opening of the vase by forming a Y shape in the neck. The Y, fixed into the opening, allows branches and stems to lean against it for support. Marbles and stones will hold stems too, and the stones look lively and fresh in water.

Bowls

If jugs have a rural flavour then bowls have a 'country house' feel about them. Inexpensive and easy mechanics are a large pinholder – 7.5cm (3in.) – set firmly in the bowl, with crumpled wire netting loosely filling the rest of the space and with the strands of wire caught securely on the pinholder. If floral foam is needed, aim to fill two-thirds of the bowl only, for it should never touch the sides of a container as it encourages plant material to syphon. Always leave space for watering and don't forget to have the foam at least 5cm (2in.) above the rim so that stems can be inserted to give a downwards flow.

Shallow containers

Shallow containers, often rectangular or irregular in shape, are suitable for water arrangements. These are definite in style and are designs where the plant material has associations with water. The plant material is restrained in amount and is usually set to one side of the shallow container in a pinholder, leaving at least half to two-thirds of the water showing. These arrangements are similar to ikebana, the Japanese style of arranging.

Water-design mechanics

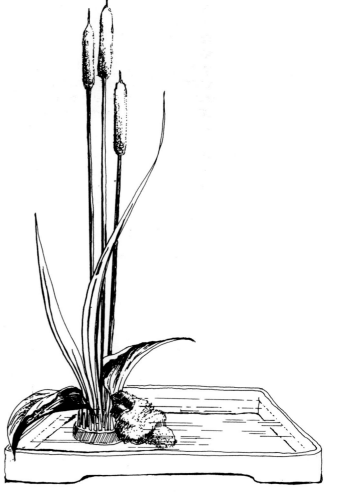

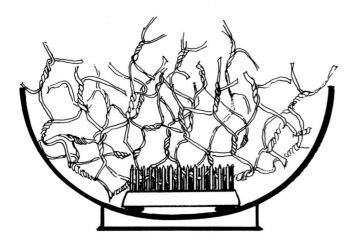

Raised designs

All sorts of containers can be used for raised designs, from the familiar cherub-stemmed container, the wine bottle filled with water with a candlecup fixed to it and the candlestick – again with the candlecup attached, to giant-sized pedestals. Pedestals are much used in large churches and cathedrals or other vast places and are mostly telescopic so their height can be adjusted. Whatever the scale of the raised container and the height of the plant material, the effect aimed at is one of gracefully flowing plant material at the sides, which is almost impossible to achieve without floral foam. Several blocks may be needed, one on top of the other, and carefully wired for the largest pedestal, while a cube of the water-retaining foam about 7.5 × 7.5 × 7.5cm (3 × 3 × 3in.) will suffice for a household container; this can sometimes be smaller, depending on the dimensions of the cup. The imperative thing is that the foam stands well above the container's rim. In the home a criss-cross of floral tape will hold the foam in place, but in larger designs it is advisable to cap the foam with 2.5cm or 5cm (1in. or 2in.) wire netting, which can be fixed to the pedestal stem with reel wire. This will take some of the weight of the stems and so prevent the foam from crumbling. Thick stems need all the support they can get.

Deep containers

It is wasteful and pointless to fill a deep container completely with floral foam. Instead, add some clean sand until two-thirds full – the ballast this gives is essential – and then rest a plastic carton on the sand. The plastic carton must be of the right diameter for the container's opening. Paint the carton to tone with the container, if necessary, and put the floral foam into it; either tape or wire it in position.

Spring
Spring flowers for a buffet table incorporating both garden and florists' flowers. The hellebores are at the seed-pod stage and so condition well; their lime-green colour adds a freshness to the overall effect. Other flowers are pink and yellow spray carnations, mauve and yellow freesias and Spiraea x arguta – bridal wealth. The mechanics are floral foam.
(Arranger Catherine Green)

65

Early autumn

Pew ends for an October wedding using cotoneaster berries, Amaranthus caudatus 'Viridis', late roses from the garden and 'Mont Blanc' lilies and cream spray carnations from the florist. Both the bride's and bridesmaids' dresses were ivory and the bridesmaids had red sashes. The whole effect was warm and seasonal. The mechanics were blocks of floral foam 10cm long × 6.5cm deep × 7.5cm wide (4in. × 2½in. × 3in.) wrapped in cling film and strengthened by a covering of 2.5cm (1in.) wire-netting. These bundles were then wired to slats of wood which protected the pews from the floral foam. They were fixed to the pews by fine wire but of course ribbon can be used for this purpose and to make hanging tails. It is easy to buy a floral foam holder for pew ends from a florist but these hold a large block and make very big arrangements.

(Arranger Pauline Mann)

Baskets

Baskets have been used as receptacles for flowers, fruit and vegetables throughout the ages. The ancient Egyptians, Greeks and Romans used them; the Chinese had many different kinds; and paintings show Flemish arrangements in baskets, all made of woven plant material. Nearer to our own times baskets were also fashioned from porcelain and silver.

Woven baskets need to have either a lining or some sort of water-holding utensil inside them before they can be used as containers. Generally, the shallower the basket the easier it is to arrange. A pinholder or floral foam in a tin, both capped and strengthened with wire netting, make suitable and simple mechanics. Use wire netting to fix the container to the basket by threading reel wire from the netting through the weave to the bottom of the basket.

Summer
Pink and white roses strikingly arranged in a fine pair of antique candle-holders and well displayed against a plain background. The mechanics are candlecups with floral foam.
(Arranger Anne Everett)

Project: a silk flower tree for summer

First cover a flower-pot of the desired size with material to tone with the chosen colour scheme.

Set a dowelling rod into the pot with concrete, taking care that it is central and vertical. When set, paint the concrete surface and the rod an appropriate colour and finish the pot with braid.

Buy two wire wreath frames, one slightly larger than the other. Separate the double rings and select three graduated in size for your tree.

Using florists' tape of a colour matching the flowers or foliage, tape the three rings and also the stems of all the flowers, foliage and components to be attached.

Fix the flowers etc. to the frames by pressing the two tacky surfaces together, and wire them using the minimum amount of wire. Cover any visible wire with tape.

Measure four lengths of ribbon and fix these first to the lowest frame, then to the middle frame and finally to the top one. Use either drawing pins or a stapler. Finally make a posy for the top of the dowelling rod.

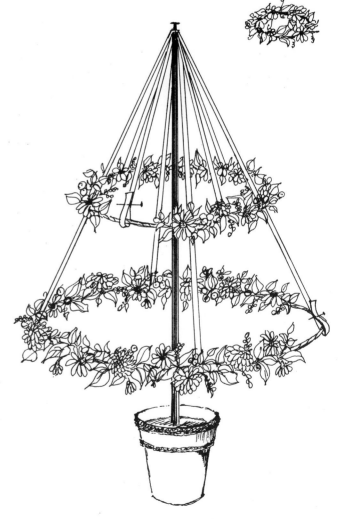

Summer
The swing tree is made of white silk flowers and bright green ribbon. There are times when flowers are scarce and artificial flowers come into their own. Using any colour flower or ribbon, this would be a pretty addition to a buffet table.
(Arranger Pauline Mann)

Project: mechanics for a cone

You will need a block of floral foam trimmed to a rough cone shape. It is important to get enough height in relation to the width to prevent it from being dumpy.

Cover first with cling film and then with a layer of wire netting to give strength.

Start by making an outline with short pieces of foliage so that you obtain a good even shape and then fill in. Some grouping of flowers will be necessary to help give rhythm to the design.

Plant material may also be recessed to create depth. Added height can be attained with the length of the top foliage.

Make sure that the foam is firmly attached to the container using either a sprog or a metal holder.

Cones need not be confined to Christmas decorations only; they lend themselves to special occasions at any time of the year.

Summer
The floral cone features the silky seed heads of the clematis 'Nellie Moser' and flowers of the Clematis tangutica. *There is also honeysuckle, cream spray carnations and small green grapes. The foliage is a mixture of* Chamaecyparis pisifera, Thalictrum adiantifolium, Viburnum tinus *and trails of clematis.*
(Arranger Pauline Mann)

7
Foliage

For the flower arranger, foliage is as important as the flowers, and what to grow takes a high priority in garden planning. But there are several factors to be considered when undertaking this pleasant task, for the area at your disposal obviously controls your choice along with the type of soil, aspect, boundaries and latitude. All of these are fundamental because they are permanent. The aim of this chapter is to describe certain shrubs, trees and plants that are greatly liked by flower arrangers but that are also decorative in the garden.

Garden Planning

When I first discovered the recommended proportion of evergreens to deciduous trees in a garden was two-thirds to one-third, I could hardly believe it. Now I realize that when this rule is followed it ensures a 'complete' look to a garden all the year round. The evergreens are the bones of the garden that result in a structured look at all times.

Planning a garden and arranging flowers have much in common. Form, line, colour, texture and the use of space are the elements of every design, and they need to be rhythmically employed so that the viewer's eye is led through the garden from feature to feature. The groupings should balance and points of emphasis are needed to give contrast. Plants should be in scale with the surroundings, and the amounts of strong colour controlled.

A catalogue from a reliable nursery is an excellent guide to selecting shrubs and trees, for it will tell you the habit of growth as well as the ultimate height and spread.

Gertrude Jekyll (1843–1932), a famous gardener, loved grey foliage plants, so many of which are indigenous to the Mediterranean. She knew how to use them in the mixed border, often with white, soft blue and pale yellow flowers.

Another notable gardener, Vita Sackville-West, was immensely imaginative with her colour combinations; her grey and white garden at Sissinghurst in Kent is legendary. My first visit there was in February – not a very propitious season – but the sight of the orchard of grey-green lichened apple trees under-planted with *Crocus tomasinianus* and C. *chrysanthus* in blues and mauves with tiny clumps of *Cyclamen coum* has stayed forever in my memory as one of the most beautiful sights I have ever seen. The grey-green was an important foil in this case, but in the average garden of today it usually isn't possible to give over a patch entirely to grey foliage. What you can do is plant grey in drifts, which will lead the eye, because pale silvery-grey leaves stand out amongst the more ordinary greens.

Variegated Foliage

Variegated foliage is of tremendous importance in both garden and flower arranging, but it should not be over-used in either. It provides lively contrast in a vase and among the shrub groupings. There are some yellow and lime-green variegated shrubs that are of a considerable brightness and need to be planted with discretion or they will dominate completely, so use them as accents at strategic points. The E*laeagnus pungens* 'Maculata', E. *pungens* 'Dicksonii', and E. x *ebbingi* 'Limelight' are especially brilliant. *Ligustrum ovalifolium* 'Auremarginatum', and L. *ovalifolium* 'Variegatum' – variegated and golden privet – can look as colourful as forsythia in the winter garden and are not to be scorned because they are common. The fairly new cultivar *Choisya ternata* 'Sundance' is very yellow, but to my mind not nearly as pleasing as the glossy ordinary one. A very bright yellow variegated shrub is *Cornus alba* 'Spaethii'. It is better planted away from its sister *Cornus alba* 'Elegantissima', which has a white variegation.

This is my personal selection of foliage that is particularly useful for arrangements.

<table>
<tr><td colspan="4">Key</td></tr>
<tr><td>A</td><td>Annual</td><td>P</td><td>Perennial</td></tr>
<tr><td>C</td><td>Climber</td><td>SE</td><td>Semi-evergreen</td></tr>
<tr><td>D</td><td>Deciduous</td><td>S</td><td>Shrub</td></tr>
<tr><td>E</td><td>Evergreen</td><td>T</td><td>Tree</td></tr>
</table>

Grey

Alchemilla alpina P

A rock plant with the reverse of the leaves a shining silver. From the front the silver bands the leaf edges. Lovely for pressing.

Artemisia P

The best species for the flower arranger is one of the least feathery and is *Artemisia ludoviciana*. This gives stems between 30cm and 90cm (12in. and 36in.) in length that condition well and do not object to floral foam.

Artemisia D or SE

The shrub-like artemisias, A. *arborescens* and A. *abrotanum* – the latter being southernwood or lad's love – are not tolerant of floral foam though they are quite reliable in water if conditioned by burning.

Ballota pseudodictamnus SE

A grey 'felt'-covered plant with individual 61cm (2ft) long sprays of rounded green-grey leaves and whorled bracts. Tiny mauve flowers emerge from the bracts; these have to be removed, along with the leaves, if you wish to dry the whorls. It is tolerant of floral foam and is a pretty and useful flower-arranging plant, remaining usable throughout most winters.

Eucalyptus gunnii E

I live in north-east England, which is chilly, so my experience of the eucalyptus is limited to E. *gunnii*, which will grow outside. In hard winters the frost cuts it down, but after being pruned to the ground in March, it has never yet failed to shoot again. This treatment keeps it as a bush, with a very purple-grey hue. The long new growth is graceful and best conditioned by burning. Mature pieces need only ordinary conditioning and glycerine well. The young leaves are rounded and the mature foliage slightly elongated.

Helichrysum angustifolium (curry plant) E

The spikey silver branches of this 91cm (3ft) shrub *do* smell of curry. In the house it looks so good in a mixed arrangement that I happily accept the slightly spicy smell, and it is long lasting in floral foam.

Hosta sieboldiana and H. sieboldiana 'Elegans' P

The glaucous species has very large 'quilted' leaves; 'Elegans' has leaves of an even deeper blue-grey. It is every flower arranger's dream to have vast quantities of these plants. I grow mine in 30cm (12in.) terracotta pots, which is the only way of preventing them from being chewed to pieces by slugs. To condition them, soak the leaves.

Lavendula spica (lavender) E

A modest and trouble-free small shrub with silver-grey lineaf, oblong leaves. It looks a little like the curry plant. From July to September the blue flowers attract bees, and it is worth growing just for this. If the flowers are to be dried for lavender bags or pot-pourri they should be cut before they are fully open and hung in bundles upside down. The foliage lasts for ages in floral foam. Bushes should be trimmed in April and also cut back after flowering. L. *spica* 'Hidcote' has deep blue flowers, and there is a dwarf variety L. *nana atropurpurea*. 'Munstead Dwarf' is listed as being a dark lavender blue and L. *vera* is 'Dutch lavender', from which lavender oil is extracted.

Phormium tenax (New Zealand flax) P

A tall architectural plant with sword-like, grey-green, ridged leaves. It needs the protection of a south-facing wall or hedge, but once established it seems hardy enough. It is spectacular for modern designs and the great leaves dry well. It will easily reach 1.8m (6ft).

Ruta graveolens 'Jackman's Blue' (rue) SE

Lacy glaucous foliage that only reaches 61cm (2ft) in height. The leaves press well for pictures and are also attractive in small mixed fresh designs. It has a sharp smell that is astringent but quite pleasant. Semi-evergreen and easy, its blue colour is essential in the garden. It is tolerant of floral foam.

Rosemarinus officinalis (rosemary) E

Valuable because of its scented leaves that may be used in cooking and because it lasts well in floral foam. It is the underside of the leaves that are the palest grey. Propagated easily from cuttings, it will attain a height of 1.8m (6ft).

Santolina chamaecyparissus (cotton lavender) E

Another small grey-leaved shrub that has been in this country a long time. This grows to about 61cm (2ft) tall and has feathery aromatic foliage. Like lavender it makes a good edging plant or dwarf hedge; it was used in this way in Tudor knot gardens. Can be put in floral foam.

Senecio laxifolius and S. greyi E

There is confusion between these two similar species, though laxifolius is said to have larger leaves but to grow to a height of only 1.2m (4ft), while greyi attains 2.4m (8ft). Both have some of the largest grey leaves to be found among our evergreens. They are pewter coloured on the surface and grey-white underneath. Trouble-free as far as cultivation goes, they do look a little tired early in the year and should be severely pruned in April to promote new growth – but leave some straggling pieces for flower

A *refreshing and stylish table display with Michaelmas daisies and a variety of foliage swathed around three white candles.* (Arranger Anne Everett)

arranging. Both species are reliable for cutting when mature, and are quite happy in floral foam.

Sorbus aria 'Lutescens' (whitebeam) T

A tree much coveted by the flower arranger for its spring foliage. When the leaves first appear it is very striking because it looks as though pale green-grey butterflies are resting on the branches. Later, the leaves turn green above but stay grey below. The flowers are clusters of white, which turn eventually to berries. The height of the mature tree is around 10m (33ft). Condition carefully.

Stachys lanata (lamb's tongue) P

The woolly grey leaves are there all the year round, though they do not look particularly attractive during the winter. Spikes of insignificant magenta flowers appear in June and July which can be dried. Because of its furry appearance, it has an interesting texture during the summer and should be placed at the front of the border. The spikes can be put in floral foam.

Red

Acer palmatum 'Atropurpureum' D

The leaves are red and purple throughout the summer. Grows to 3.6m (12ft) high.

Acer palmatum 'Atropurpureum Dissectum' D

The Japanese maples are numerous and all have outstanding autumn colour. 'Dissectum' forms a low, rounded bush about 1m (3ft) in height.

Atriplex hortensis (mountain spinach) A

A true flower arranger's plant, which fruits in dock-like spikes that can be glycerined. Once introduced into the garden, it will seed itself.

Berberis thunbergii 'Atropurpurea' and 'Rose Glow' D S

Deep red leaves, with those of 'Rose Glow' splashed with a white variegation. Not the easiest shrub to condition and it is best to burn the stem ends. It does not like floral foam.

Cotinus coggygria (smoke tree) D S

This is one of the best red-leaved shrubs, even though the foliage must be mature before it is used in a flower arrangement. Its season isn't all that long because of this, being July to October, though it can be cut until November. Once the foliage has matured it lasts for weeks in water or even in floral foam. A fully grown bush can reach a height of 3m (10ft). C. *coggygria* 'Notcutt's Variety' is slightly smaller.

Heuchera micrantha diversifolia 'Palace purple' P

The heucheras are herbaceous perennials that keep their leaves during the winter. They are worth their weight in gold and are perfect for the small garden. The above named variety has deep red heart-shaped leaves that are lighter on the reverse measuring between 5cm and 7.6cm (2in. and 3in.) across.

Malus (Flowering crab) D

There are several purple-leaved crabs, which all have red flowers. Malus 'Profusion' attains 6m (20ft).

Phormium tenax 'Purpureum' and 'Bronze baby' P

This is a coppery-red dwarf of 60cm (2ft). 'Dazzler' is a reddish brown variety of 60cm–80cm (2ft–2¾ft). This plant has architectural sword-like leaves. The above varieties, with their reddish variegations, are not as hardy as the plain species but they can be grown outside in pots during the summer and be protected in a greenhouse during the winter. Can be put in floral foam.

Prunus cerasifera 'Pissardii' T

This is the purple-leaved plum whose flowers come early on its bare branches. It grows to a height of 7m (23ft). Prunus x *blireiana* has coppery-purple foliage and is smaller – 3.6m (12ft). Mature foliage can be put in floral foam, but care should be taken with conditioning.

Rosa rubrifolia D S

An easy-to-cultivate species rose that is a must for the flower arranger. Its silvery-purple foliage grows in graceful arching sprays. It seldom reaches a greater height than 1.8m (6ft). It can be put in floral foam, but make sure you condition it well first.

Vitis vinifera 'Purpurea' (ornamental vine) P

These vines are not grown for their grapes but for their beautiful foliage. They will need some support. Burn the stem ends before giving a long spell in water. They prefer water to floral foam.

Other deciduous shrubs and trees

Acer campestre 'Flamingo' D

This may be grown as either a shrub or small tree and will reach 2m–3m (6½ft–10ft) or 3m–4m (10ft–13ft) respectively. The leaves are a bright pink at first, turning to green with white and pink variegations.

Acer negundo 'Aureum' D

'Aureum' has bright golden-yellow leaves, and A. 'Variegatum' has leaves with white margins. You can pick long sprays of foliage, but be sure to burn the stem ends before arranging.

Acer palmatum D

Will attain a height of 3m (10ft). It has five or seven-lobed leaves that press well.

All acers (maples) have greeny-yellow flowers which are most eye-catching for they appear on the bare branches. There are other acers with unusual barks which add colour and interest to the winter garden.

Acer pseudoplatanus 'Brilliantissimum' D

A slow-growing, mop-headed tree recommended for its wonderful spring leaf colour, which is a shrimp pink that turns to a pale bronze before becoming a more mundane green. It will reach a height of 2m–3m (6½ft–10ft).

Arum italicum 'Pictum' P

A cultivated version of lords and ladies. One of the arrangers' favourite larger leaves. They come through the soil in autumn and are at their best in the early spring, though they last well into the early summer. The leaves are arrow-shaped, criss-crossed with light-coloured veining. Condition by floating, but to stop the stems from curling, gently tie them to a straight stick or put the stems into a tube during their immersion.

Bergenia P

A real stand-by throughout the year. There are several species to choose from but the one with the best shape is B. *cordifolia* with heart-shaped leaves. B. *cordifolia purpurea*'s leaves turn purplish in winter whilst B. 'Evening Glow' has maroon foliage, as has B. 'Sunningdale'. Reddish or pink flowers appear from March to May, but it is the leaves that are so valuable, as ground cover and for picking. Condition by soaking (floating). Can be put in floral foam.

Buxus sempervirens E

The common box has plain, shiny dark green leaves, but there are two varieties that are slightly more colourful: B. 'Aurea Marginata' with a yellow-edged leaf, and B. 'Latifolia Maculata' which has leaves streaked with yellow. Box goes well in foliage designs and in swags and garlands. It glycerines well, turning to a pale tobacco brown – perhaps one of its greatest merits.

Camellia japonica E

Although often thought of as delicate, the numerous varieties have proved to be hardy, though damage occurs when they are planted in windy, open positions or facing east where the sun will scorch the frosted flowers and leaf tips before they have had time to thaw out naturally. They need acid soil and without it should be given doses of fertilizer. The foliage is beautifully glossy; it lasts for weeks when cut. Leaves glycerine to a very dark brown colour.

Cornus D S

The dogwoods are easy to grow. Two of them are strikingly colourful. I think the more desirable is *Cornus alba* 'Siberica', which has pale green leaves with silver-white markings. It makes a compact bush of about 1.5m (4ft). *Cornus alba* 'Elegantissima' has a looser habit of growth and is slightly taller.

Danae racemosa (Ruscus racemosus) E

This is of great value to the flower arranger. Its foliage is sold in florists' as ruscus. It grows in arching stems, bearing narrow, pointed, elongated leaves of a fresh, shiny green, which last a long time in water and also glycerine successfully, turning a light brown. This plant is low growing and can be put in floral foam.

Elaeagnus pungens 'Maculata' E

A favourite with flower arrangers and gardeners alike. A shrub with very vivid yellow variegation that needs careful placing in the garden. 'Maculata' has leaves with bright golden centres; it is neat in its habit, reaching about 1.5m (5ft) in height. E. x *ebbingei* 'Limelight' is a fast grower with yellow leaf centres; it grows taller to 9m (30ft). E. x *ebbingei* 'Gilt Edge' has a self explanatory name. It grows to 1.8m (6ft). All the varieties have the characteristic 'cat's nose'-textured stem and leaf reverse. They condition easily and well and can be put in floral foam.

Escallonia SE

In some parts of Britain or during hard winters, escallonias are not fully evergreen. The arching branches are a joy to flower arrangers with or without their flowers, but choose a variety recommended for its graceful growth – e.g. E. x *Edinensis*, E. 'Slieve Donard', E. 'Donard Brilliance' and E. 'Donard Seedling'. The height of these is roughly 1.8m (6ft).

Euonymus E

It is the evergreen species of this genus that are so important to both the gardener and the arranger. Most of these are low growing and so furnish the front of the border throughout the year with their small, glossy and interestingly variegated leaves. There are several to choose from, all trouble free, if rather slow growing (as most variegated plants are). One variety, planted with some dwarf conifers or plain-leaved shrubs, 'lifts' the group effectively. Tremendously long-lasting when cut, this shrub is ideal for swags and garlands. The varieties E. *radicans* 'Silver Queen', and E. *radicans* 'Emerald 'n' Gold' are perhaps the best known, though there are several others fairly alike but with a less prostrate growth habit (*radicans* means 'creeping' or 'prostrate'). These low growing specimens can be trained to climb up walls, with some support. Can be put in floral foam.

Fatshedera lizei E

A cross between F*atsia japonica* 'Moserin' and H*edera helix hibernica*, the parentage is obvious in the leaf. Usually grown as a house-plant, it will also thrive outside, though the form 'Variegata' is for indoors only. The leaves of both hardy and indoor varieties condition easily and last well. They also glycerine, turning a surprising cream colour, which makes them attractive for swags. Can be put in floral foam.

Fatsia japonica E

A shrub on a large scale because of the size of its palmate five- or seven-lobed leaves, which can be enormous or as small as 12.7cm (5in.) in diameter. It needs some shelter in the garden and is said to prefer shade. It thrives on annual doses of fertilizer. The leaves are wonderful for the arranger, both for modern and large traditional designs. They last for weeks when cut. They also glycerine beautifully, but for this process the stems need to be supported with soft wood strips, for they are weak at the point where the stem joins the leaf. An alternative way of glycerining is to submerge the entire leaf in a vessel large enough for the leaf to lie flat. Height 1.5m–3m (5ft–10ft). Can be put in floral foam.

Garrya elliptica E

Dark green on the surface, the leaves are greyish and felty beneath. The male plants produce the best catkins in late winter and early spring; at a distance, these look rather like thick cobwebs, and can be quite spectacular. The foliage is close on the stems and therefore makes a good groundwork for swags and garlands. A height of 3m (10ft) is usual when grown against a wall. It lasts for weeks when cut and can be put in floral foam.

Griselinia littoralis E

In the warmer south and west of Britain this shrub can grow to a height of 3m (10ft). It is one of the plants that thrives at the sea-side. Its ovate, fleshy leaves are an unusual pale green. The variegated version, G. *littoralis* 'Variegata' is less hardy but has a pleasing soft pale yellow edge to the leaves. Because of the soft green of the foliage and its delicate variegation, this shrub should not be planted in a position where it is in competition with the brasher things such as *Elaeagnus pungens*, *Cornus alba* 'Spaethii', the gold variegated euonymus or golden privet, for these will detract from its gentle colouring. Can be put in floral foam.

Hedera E

There are not many species of ivy but lots of cultivars, especially of *Hedera helix*, the tree ivy native to Britain. All ivies are climbers so when they find support they go upwards, clinging on to house, fence, tree or wall with their short stem suckers. They are more desirable for flower arrangers than gardeners perhaps, for the trailing stems and winter berries are particularly sought after for winter designs. *H. canariensis* 'Variegata', with its creamy variegation and shiny wine-red stems, and *H. colchica dentata* 'Variegata' with bright yellow splashes and edges on the glossy, and often very large leaves, are commonly seen climbing over walls and fences. *Hedera* 'Buttercup' has greeny-yellow rounded leaves and is far less rampant than *H. colchica*. *Hedera* 'Goldheart', with bright red stems, is another ivy frequently seen; though striking in appearance it has a very stiff growth habit. All ivies are hardy, though a sharp winter can scorch them badly. Young growth is difficult to condition, but when mature they are all indestructible and completely happy in floral foam.

Hosta P

H. 'Honeybells', is plain with lanceolate leaves of an unusual yellow-green, which keep their colour for the entire summer. Many hostas fade and lose their variegation as the summer progresses. *H. fortunei* 'Albopicta' has leaves marbled with different greens and yellows and is beautiful until July when its colours begin to fade. *H. undulata* has unmistakable twisty leaves with bold patches of white. 'Thomas Hogg' has a slightly smoother surface than most and a creamy margin; this is a very reliable plant and keeps going throughout the season. *H. fortunei* 'Aureo-marginata' is deeply quilted and has a narrow yellow edge.

Iris foetidissima (Gladdon) P

This is one of the plants I would really miss, for the plain green leaves are available all through the winter. The flowers are insignificant but result in wonderful fat seedpods that contain bright orange seeds; these should be picked just before they open and be put to dry in a warm place. When dry they can be sprayed with hair lacquer or a clear picture varnish to prevent them from withering and falling. However, they will drop eventually whatever you do, but the empty seed cases are well worth preserving for use in dried swags and garlands.

Iris pseudacorus 'Variegata' P

This is a true water iris which, if planted near a lake or stream, will reach a height of 1.5m (5ft). In the border its height is restricted to 60cm (2ft). The foliage is striped with yellow.

Ligustrum ovalifolium 'Aureo-marginatum' (golden privet) SE

Some people dislike privet, and certainly the ordinary green one makes a tyrannical hedge, demanding to be cut three times during the summer and denuding the soil of nutrients! However, the golden privet should be left to grow freely. In a bad winter it may loose its leaves. Can be put in floral foam.

Mahonia E

There are two members of this genus that I would miss if they were not in my garden: the common *M. aquifolium* and *M. japonica* (or *bealei*). The former is an accommodating shrub with leaves that turn bronze in the winter months. *M. japonica* has great, glossy dark green pinnate leaves and a lily-of-the-valley scented yellow flower that grows in a raceme during the winter. This species may grow to a height of 1.8m (6ft). Both forms glycerine well, turning a dark brown and lasting for ever! Completely tolerant of floral foam.

Mentha (mint) P

All the mints are invasive in the garden. They can be planted in a bucket to prevent the roots from spreading. *M. rotundifolia* 'Variegata' has bright green hairy leaves with creamy-white markings. It is quite delightful in colour although it needs careful conditioning, even when it's mature. The leaves of *M.x gentilis* 'Variegata' are smoother than those of *rotundifolia*, and its yellow variegations less pronounced; it is hard to condition, but it is worth growing, if only for the scent when crushed. Both species are better in water than in floral foam.

Pachysandra terminalis E

A ground cover plant that grows best in the shade. There is a variegated form which, naturally, grows less strongly, as do all variegated plants because the manufacture of food takes longer when all the leaf is not green. Pachysandra is valuable to the arranger because it grows in rosettes, always a sought-after form, especially for garlands, cones and swags. It conditions well and can be put in floral foam. It also glycerines to a dark brown.

Philadelphus coronarius 'Aureus' D S

The flower arranger removes the foliage from other philadelphus but grows this species for its very yellow leaves alone. In flower it looks unattractive. Although it is at its brightest in early summer, it maintains its colour throughout the season. Can be put in floral foam.

Phormium tenax (New Zealand flax) E

P. tenax 'Variegatum' has leaves striped with different shades of green outlined with wider bands of cream. The amount of variegation varies, and no two plants are exactly the same. *P. cookianum* 'Cream Delight' is a compact grower with a cream band in the centre of the leaves, height 1m (3ft). Some protection may be required during the winter. All the phormium leaves dry well.

Pittosporum tenuifolium E

One of the foliages most commonly available from the florist. It makes a dense shrub of small, shiny evergreen leaves with wavy margins. *P. x* 'Garnettii' has larger leaves with white edges and is reported to be hardier than the other white variegated form, *P. tenuifolium* 'Silver Queen'. All grow to about 3m (10ft). Can be put in floral foam and it also glycerines well, turning a mid-brown.

Rubus cockburnianus D S

The 'white-washed' bramble with leaves that are white underneath and have white stems. Attractive both in summer and especially in winter. *Rubus tricolour* grows quickly and is a ground cover plant with exceptionally glossy and textured leaves on long prostrate stems covered with red furry bristles. Long lasting and can be put in floral foam.

Sambucus racemosa 'Plumosa Aurea' D S

Deeply-cut foliage which is a brilliant green-yellow early in the season, turning to gold later. About 2m (6½ft) high. It needs careful conditioning and prefers water.

Skimmia x 'Foremanii' E

'Foremanii' is considered the best female form but it must be accompanied by a male (S. *peevesiana* 'Rubella' or S. *japonica* 'Fragrans') in order to berry. Skimmias are shade lovers and prefer an acid soil. They seldom grow much more than 1m (3ft) high and so need to be planted towards the front of the border so that their large, bright red berries will show in winter. Skimmia glycerines well and lasts a long while in floral foam.

Thalictrum adiantifolium P

Numerous small leaflets give this plant the appearance of the maidenhair fern. It is very dainty and feathery and is lovely for summer flower arrangements. It glycerines easily and quickly, turning a mid-brown. Can be put in floral foam.

Viburnum tinus and *V. tinus* 'Variegatum' S

I particularly cherish any shrub or plant that flowers during the winter months, and the V*iburnum tinus* starts to open its pinky-white blossoms in November, continuing to flower well into spring. The dark green leaves last a long time in floral foam as do those of the variegated form, V. *tinus* 'Variegatum'. This has lighter, almost olive green, leaves banded with pale yellow and flowers similar to the plain leaved *tinus*. The variegated one is a first class inhabitant of the garden, both for size and colour. Height about 1.8m (5ft) when fully grown.

Vinca major 'Variegata' E

Flower arrangers love vinca because of its trailing habit. It has good yellow markings. It needs a long soak before it is used in floral foam, otherwise the growing ends of sprays tend to flag. Good ground cover.

Weigela florida 'Variegata' D S

Although this shrub has pretty pale pink flowers in May, it is its foliage that is so attractive and valuable. Superficially it resembles *Cornus alba siberica* 'Variegata', but the weigela makes a more compact bush and has better shaped branches for use in flower arranging. The green is also brighter and it conditions more easily. The variegation is creamy-yellow. Maximum height 1.8m (6ft). Condition for 36 hours if possible.

Winter
Brass candlesticks and gold candles enliven this seasonal design of evergreens. The plant material includes Hedera colchica 'Sulphur Heart', Phormium tenax, Ilex aquifolium 'Silver Queen', Ilex altaclarensis 'Golden King' and Hedera colchica 'Denata Variegata'. (Arranger Janet Hayton)

Appendix:
Flowers through the Seasons

Florists' flowers available throughout the year

Alstroemeria (Peruvian lily)
Anemone
Anthurium
Bouvardia
Carnation and spray carnation
Chrysanthemum
Freesia
Gerbera (barberton daisy)
Gladioli (sword lily)
Gypsophila (baby's breath)
Hippeastrum
Iris
Liatris (gayfeather)
Lily
Orchid
Protea
Rose
Strelitzia (bird of paradise flower)

Key

A	Annual
B	Biennial
BU	Bulb
D	Deciduous
E	Evergreen
HHA	Half-hardy annual
P	Perennial
SE	Semi-evergreen
R	Rhizome
SH	Shrub
T	Tree
TU	Tuber

Spring

Pinks and Reds

	Plant	Conditioning and availability
TU	Anemone St Brigid and de Caen	Water. Buy in bud when showing colour and fat
SH	Camellia	Woody stem conditioning. Water. Florists' or gardens
SH	*Chaenomeles* (Quince)	Woody stem conditioning. Floral foam. Gardens
P	*Helleborus orientalis*	Water. Gardens
BU	Hyacinthus	All bulbs are best in water. Gardens, markets and florists'
T	*Prunus triloba*	Woody stem conditioning. Floral foam. Florists' and gardens
SH	*Ribes* (Flowering currant)	May be forced into flower by being brought into the house from December onwards. Floral foam
BU	Tulipa	Water is best, but floral foam tolerant. Florists' and markets

White and greenish white

	Plant	Conditioning and availability
T	*Amelanchier canadensis* (snowy mesipilus)	Woody stem conditioning. One of the earliest trees to blossom. Floral foam, though water is better. Gardens
SH	*Camellia japonica* 'Alba Simplex'	Woody stem conditioning. Water. Florists' or gardens
BU	Narcissus 'Mount Hood', 'Snowshill', 'Cantatrice'	Water is best
P	*Helleborus foetidus* *Helleborus corsicus*	Water. Gardens
BU	Hyacinth	All bulb flowers are best in water. Gardens, markets and florists'
SH	*Spiraea* x *arguta* (bridal wreath)	Flowers in May – or earlier in the south. Defoliate. The woody stems are very fine but should be split. Better in water
BU	Tulipa	Water is best. Florists' and markets
SH	*Virburnum opulus* 'Sterile'	Defoliate. Condition thoroughly giving woody stem treatment. Water. Florists' or gardens

Spring

A 'dish garden' can be made at any time of the year but it is especially suitable in spring when the first flowering shrubs will supply a tall branch of blossom and there are so many small flowers in the garden to be grouped to fill the dish. The effect is usually polychromatic. In this arrangement the forsythia and irises give the necessary height; the early double tulips 'Apple Blossom' have good round shapes to contrast with the smaller flowers which include 'Peeping Tom' daffodils, Helleborus foetidus and corsicus, heathers, polyanthus and some Arum italicum 'Pictum' leaves. The container is a large shallow grey dish in which there are several pinholders for the various placements. Moss can be used to fill any gaps.
(Arranger Pauline Mann)

Spring

A *graceful, refreshing arrangement of some of the most beautiful spring flowers. Dark blue irises complement pale yellow daffodils and golden yellow jonquils. Pink tulips and gypsophila are interspersed.* (Arranger Janet Hayton)

Blue and purple

Plant		Conditioning and availability
BU	Chionodoxa	Water. Gardens
BU	Hyacinthus	Water. Florists' and markets
BU	Iris	Water though floral foam tolerant. Florists' and markets
B	Lunaria (honesty)	Floral foam. Gardens
B	Matthiola (Brompton stock)	Remove most of the leaves. Split stem. Floral foam
BU	Muscari (grape hyacinth)	Water. Gardens
B	Myosotis (forget-me-not)	Water. Gardens
P	*Primula denticulata*	Water. Gardens
BU	Scilla	Water. Gardens
P	Viola (pansy)	Water. Gardens
P	Violet	Water. Float to condition and spray frequently. Florists' and markets

Yellow and orange

Plant		Conditioning and availability
P	Auricula, polyanthus and *Primula vulgaris* (primrose)	Water and spray
SH	Chaenomeles (quince)	Woody stem conditioning. Floral foam. Garden material
SH	Forsythia	May be forced into flower by being brought into the house from December onwards. Floral foam tolerant though better in water. Florists' stock forced branches early in the year. Gardens
BU	*Fritillaria imperialis* (crown imperial)	Floral foam tolerant but better in water
BU	Iris	Water, though floral foam tolerant. Florists' and markets
SH	*Kerria japonica* and 'Pleniflora'	Woody stem conditioning. Floral foam
BU	Narcissus (daffodil)	Water. Gardens and florists'
P	Trollius	Water
BU	Tulipa	Water is best but floral foam tolerant. Florists' and markets

Early summer

Blue and purple

Plant		Conditioning and availability
P	Anchusa	Water
P	Aquilegia (columbine)	Floral foam
SH	Clematis	Float flowers and leaves separately for two hours. Water
P	Nepeta (catmint)	Floral foam
P	Polemonium (Jacob's ladder)	Floral foam
TU	Iris (bearded)	Floral foam
SH	Syringa (lilac)	Defoliate. Pick when the flowers are out, not in bud. Water. Florists' and gardens

Yellow and Orange

Plant		Conditioning and availability
P	Aquilegia	Floral foam
P	Doronicum (leopard's bane)	Water
P	Euphorbia polychroma, E. robbiae, E. wulfenii, E. griffithii 'Fireglow'	Floral foam if the stem ends are burnt
SH	Lonicera	Woody stem conditioning

Early summer
The slightly mauve-pink and orange are adjacent on the colour wheel. They provide quite a sharp combination, much liked by flower arrangers, that looks equally at ease in pink, peach or green colour schemes. The blossom is Prunus 'Kanzan', the tulips are the Darwin 'Olympic Flame'; the stocks are blue-red. The background of pale green shows up the arrangement well. The container holds floral foam and is a copper urn mounted on a plinth of the same shade.
(Arranger Pauline Mann)

High summer

Pink and red

	Plant	Conditioning and availability
BU	Allium	Floral foam
A	*Amaranthus caudatus* (love-lies-bleeding)	Floral foam. Will glycerine or dry. Florists' and markets
P	Astilbe	Water. Gardens
A	Cosmos	Floral foam. Florists' and markets
A	*Delphinium consolida* (larkspur)	Floral foam. Will dry. Florists' and markets
P	*Dicentra spectabilis* (bleeding heart)	Floral foam. Gardens
SH	Escallonia	Defoliate a little. Floral foam. Gardens
P	*Heuchera sanguinea* (coral flower)	Floral foam. Gardens
A	Lathyrus (sweet pea)	Floral foam. Florists' and markets
A	Lavatera (annual mallow)	Floral foam. Florists' and markets
SH	*Leycesteria formosa*	Defoliate. Floral foam. Gardens
A	Nicotiana (tobacco plant)	Florsts' and markets
P	*Paeonia lactiflora* 'Sarah Bernhardt', 'William Cranfield', 'Bowl of Beauty' and many others	Pick when buds are opening. Floral foam. Florists' will have paeonies sometimes, but usually they are grown by the flower arranger
P	Phlox – many	Floral foam but best in water
SH	Rosa (rose)	Defoliate a little. Woody stem conditioning
SH	*Spiraea bumalda* 'Anthony Waterer' S. *billardii*	Woody stem conditioning. Defoliate a little. Water
SH	*Weigela florida* 'Variegata'	Weigela flowers are not long-lived when picked, but the variegated foliage of this species is very attractive in flower arrangements. Pick when mature and give woody stem treatment

Summer

Arrangement in a pottery container, using the gentlest of early pink tints. The subtle pinks and cream of the roses and paeonies harmonize well with the delicate grey foliage of Rosa rubrifolia.
(Arranger Pauline Mann)

85

White and green-white

	Plant	Conditioning and availability
P	Achillea (Yarrow) 'The Pearl' and 'Perry's White'	Long lasting clusters of white flowers. Will dry. Floral foam. Florists'
P	*Achemilla mollis* (lady's mantle)	Yellow-green flowers that will dry or glycerine. Gardens
A	*Amaranthus caudatus* 'Viridis' (love-lies-bleeding)	Long lasting tails of tiny green flowers that will dry and also glycerine. Floral foam. Garden material though sometimes found in markets
P	*Anemone japonica* (windflower) 'White Giant', 'Louise Uhink', 'Honorine Jobert'	Beatiful late summer flowers from the herbaceous border. They will only last in water
P	Aquilegia (columbine) 'Snow Queen'	Floral foam
P	*Campanula persicifolia*, 'Snowdrift'. 'Pantiflora Alba'. (bellflower)	Floral foam
SH	*Choisya ternata* (mexican orange)	A shrub with shiny evergreen leaves and sweet scented white flowers in May. The foliage turns an attractive cream when glycerined. Gardens
SH	*Deutzia scabra* 'Plena'	Defoliate. Woody stem conditioning. Floral foam. Gardens
P	*Dicentra spectabilis* (bleeding heart)	Floral foam. Gardens
B	Digitalis (foxglove)	Floral foam. Pick when the lower flowers are open. Gardens
P	Heuchera 'Pearl Drops', 'Green finch'	Floral foam. Gardens
A	Lathyrus (sweet pea)	Floral foam. Florists' and gardens
SH	Syringa (lilac)	Defoliate. Pick when the flowers are out, not in bud. Water. Florists' and gardens
BU	Lilium – candidum, ragale, auratum and many hybrids	These will last well when cut and are tolerant of floral foam. Florists have a great variety
HHA	*Molucella laevis* (bells of Ireland)	Enormously popular with flower arrangers. The green bracts will both glycerine or dry and turn a pale cream. Floral foam
HHA	*Nicotiana alata* and 'Lime Green'	Sweetly scented. Floral foam. Somtimes florists' have this, but it is usually garden grown
P	*Paeonia lactiflora* 'White Wings' and *Paeonia officinalis* 'Alba-plena'	Pick when buds are opening. Floral foam. Florists will have paeonies somtimes, but usually they are grown by flower arranger
P	*Papaver orientale* (oriental poppy) 'Perry's White	Must be picked in bud and have the stem burnt. Best in water
SH	Philadelphus (mock orange) Several varieties and cultivars	Defoliate. Woody stem conditioning. Very sweetly scented. Floral foam tolerant but best in water. Florists' will have it in season
P	Phlox 'White Admiral'	Floral foam but best in water
P	Polygonatum (Solomon's Seal)	Arching stems bear green leaves and small white flowers in May. After flowering the leaves glycerine well, and become a pleasant cream. Floral foam
TU	*Ranunculus asiaticus*	Ranunculus are varied in colour, but there are some white ones. They are long lasting and tolerate floral foam. Florists stock them during the early summer
SH	*Spiraea x arguta* (bridal wreath) *Spiraea vanhouttei*	S. x *arguta* flowers in May and S. *vanhouttei* several weeks later. Defoliate. The woody stems are very fine but should be split. Floral foam but better in water
HHA	Zinnia 'Envy'	To prevent the stems from bending push a wire through the entire length

Summer
New Dawn and Iceberg roses arranged in a white basket make a pleasing,
delicate arrangement.
(Arranger Pauline Mann)

Blue and purple

Plant		Conditioning and availability
BU	Agapanthus	Floral foam
BU	Allium	Floral foam
BU	Brodiaea	Floral foam
P	Campanula 'Telham Beauty'	Floral foam
A	*Centaurea cyanus* (cornflower)	Floral foam
SH	Clematis	Float flowers and leaves separately for two hours. Water
A	*Delphinium consolida* (larkspur)	Floral foam
P	*Delphinium elatum*	Needs very thorough conditioning if it is to be placed in floral foam
P	Echinops (globe thistle)	Floral foam
P	Eryngium (sea holly)	Floral foam
SH	Hydrangea	Will condition when it is really mature. Water
A	Lathyrus (sweet pea)	Floral foam
A	*Nigella damascena* (love-in-a-mist)	Floral foam
P	Phlox	Will tolerate floral foam but is best in water
P	Scabiosa (scabious)	Will tolerate floral foam but is best in water
P	Veronica	Water

Yellow and orange

Plant		Conditioning and availability
P	*Achillea filipendulina*	Floral foam tolerant when mature. Will dry
P	Coreopsis	Floral foam
TU	Dahlia	Floral foam
P	*Gaillardia aristata*	Floral foam
BU	Gladioli – garden grown	Floral foam
P	Helenium	Floral foam
P	*Helianthus decapetalus* (sunflower)	Floral foam
P	*Heliopsis scabra*	Condition well. Floral foam
P	Inula	Floral foam
P	*Kniphofia uvaria* (red hot poker)	Floral foam
BU	Lilium (lily)	Floral foam
SH	Lonicera	Woody stem conditioning
A&P	*Rudbeckia nitida* R. 'Goldsturm' R. *hirta* 'Irish Eyes', 'Marmalade'	Water
P	Verbascum	Water

Summer

A Victorian arrangement in a silver and glass epergne. Small flowers are used in shades of blue and pink and include Doris pinks, spray pink roses, gypsophila, brodia and adiantum fern.
(Arranger Elizabeth Duffield)

Autumn

Pink and red

Plant		Conditioning and availability
P	Chrysanthemum	Conditioning for hard stems. Defoliate a little. Floral foam
SH	Cotoneaster 'Cornubia'	Woody stem conditioning. Defoliate – partly in order to allow the berries to be seen. Floral foam
TU	Dahlia	Floral foam
BU	Nerine	Floral foam
SH	*Pyracantha atalantioides* P. 'Watereri'	Treat like Cotoneaster. Floral foam
SH	Rose hips	Floral foam. Spray with hair lacquer or clear varnish to prevent them from shrivelling too quickly
TU	Schizostylis	Floral foam
SH	*Stranvaesia davidiana*	Wood stem conditioning. Floral foam
SH	*Viburnum fragrans, V. bodnantense, V. tinus*	V. *tinus* needs some defoliating in order to allow the flowers to show

Orange and yellow

Plant		Conditioning and availability
P	Chrysanthemum	These are available throughout the year at the florists', but the garden varieties are most attractive with many new cultivars to choose from. Floral foam tolerant and long lasting. Take off all the lower leaves and give the conditioning necessary for hard stems
SH	*Clematis tangutica*	Small yellow bell-like flowers which last better than the large hybrid flowers, and may even be put in floral foam. Float to condition. The delicate hairy seedheads will glycerine
SH	*Cotoneaster franchetii* (orange) C. x *Rothschildianus* (yellow)	Woody stem conditioning. Floral foam tolerant. Defoliate enough to allow the berries to be seen
TU	Dahlia	Floral foam tolerant. These valuable colourful flowers often last well into autumn – as long as there are no frosts
P	*Physalis alkakengi, P. franchetii* (Chinese lanterns)	Will dry. Floral foam
SH	Pyracantha 'Orange Glow' P. *atalantioides* 'Aurea' P. *rogersiana* "Flava'	The two latter pyracantha have yellow berries. Remove leaves to allow berries to be seen. Floral foam. Woody stem conditioning
T	Sorbus 'Joseph Rock'	This cultivar has yellow berries. To prevent berries from shrivelling too quickly spray them with hair lacquer or some clear fixative. Condition them in sugar water

Autumn

A feeling of warmth is created by the advancing adjacent hues in the autumn church arrangement. The copper container holds floral foam for the long stems of the partly defoliated cotoneaster berries, 'Enchantment' lilies, gerbera 'Terrakim' and yellow chrysanthemums. The design shows up well against the stone.
(Arranger Janet Hayton)

Winter

Winter-flowering plants, trees and shrubs give me more pleasure than those of any other season – at least that is how I feel during the dark months, though I can't deny the excitement of re-discovering scents and colours of all sorts of flowers each time they make their annual reappearance.

The following short list is of shrubs, trees and plants that flower intermittently from November onwards. In some cases the number of flowers depends on the amount of sunshine they have had during the previous summer, and also upon the winter temperature.

I have not included anything exotic that needs special protection and I am sure that on the west coast of Britain and in the south the list would be longer. (I have seen camellias in full flower in Cornwall in February.) Mine is a catalogue of plants that give me great satisfaction and grow in my wet and exposed garden in north east England, and if they grow for me they will grow for you too.

Plant		Conditioning and availability
SH	Cotoneaster	The hybrid 'Cornubia' holds its *red* berries well into the spring. Floral foam. Woody stem conditioning
SH	*Daphne mezereum*	Flowers from pale *mauvish pink* to *purplish-red*. 'Alba' is a *white* flowered form. Cut sparingly. Water
SH	*Garrya elliptica*	Dark green leathery evergreen foliage with winter catkins of *silvery grey* turning to *pale yellow*. Buy 'James Roof' if possible. Floral foam. Long lasting. Will glycerine. Woody stem conditioning
SH	*Hamamelis mollis*	The variety 'Pallida' is recommended. It has *pale yellow* flowers. Water. Cut sparingly for all the witch hazels are slow growing and are chiefly for interest in the garden rather than for flower arranging. Woody stem conditioning
P	Hellebores	These valuable plants are somewhat erratic in their flowering. I have listed them in their normal order of blooming:
P	*Helleborus niger*	This is commonly called the Christmas rose. 'Potter's Wheel' is a strong cultivar. White flowers. Leaves evergreen
P	*Helleborus atrorubens*	Deciduous. *Plum-coloured flowers.* January–February
P	*Helleborus foetidus*	Attractive lanceolate evergreen leaves. The flowers are green blotched with purple, and are borne in panicles; they are small compared to the other helleborus flowers
P	*Helleborus corsicus*	Evergreen. *Lime green* flowers carried in panicles up to 5cm (2ft) across
P	*Helleborus orientalis*	Known as the lenten rose. Evergreen. The flowers vary in colour from *greenish-white* through *pale to darker pink.*
		There are many other species of helleborus. All need special conditioning (see page 00) and all unfailingly last a long time after their seed-pods have formed. *Foetidus* and *corsicus* will provide the flower arranger with *lime-green* flowers (which are in fact bracts) until June, if left on the plant
R	*Iris stylosa*	This delicate little iris is also known as I. *unguicularis* or the Algerian iris. *Lavender-lilac* flowers with *yellow* and *black* markings. Strap-like evergreen leaves. Good winter flowering depends upon the rhizomes being thoroughly baked by the previous summer's sun, and also by being planted in a sunny position in well-drained poorish soil. They are not averse to some lime. The flowers should be gently pulled from the plant, not cut. Pick in tight bud and enjoy watching them open in water. Flowers from December–March
SH	*Jasminum nudiflorum*	A familiar deciduous shrub that produces bright *yellow* flowers from November to March depending on the weather. Invaluable both as a cut flower and for colour in the garden. Floral foam. Woody stem conditioning

Winter

The white vase, the two white pots and the white basket holding a small leafed begonia accentuate the warm coral background as well as tying up with the white chrysanthemums. The mechanics are crumpled wire-netting and a pinholder in the bottom of the china basket.
(Arranger Pauline Mann)

Winter

The theme of this design is: 'Windswept in the Grip of Winter'. The contorted/twisted effect of the hazel Corylus contorta, gives the feeling of movement as does the copper tubing which blends so harmoniously with the red gerberas which in turn carry the whirlwind effect through the tunnel.
(Arranger Joyce Monks)

SH	*Mahonia japonica,* M. *bealei* M. 'Charity'	These three mahonias have stems of strong, flat, holly-like leaves growing opposite to each other. Evergreen. Glycerines well. All three bear winter racemes of *yellow* lily-of-the-valley scented flowers. The leaves are floral foam tolerant, but the flowers need water
T	*Prunus subhirtella* 'Autumnalis'	*Pale pink* blossom on bare winter branches opens during mild spells. Woody stem conditioning. Floral foam tolerant
SH	Pyracantha	*Orange* berries throughout the winter. Woody stem conditioning. Floral foam tolerant
SH	Rhododendron	Low growing, semi-evergreen R. *praecox* is covered with *lilac* flowers February to March
SH	*Skimmia japonica*	Evergreen. For good berries choose a bisexual variety; S. *reevesiana* is recommended. Needs acid soil. Floral foam. Woody stem conditioning
SH	*Symphoricarpus albus*	'Laevigatus' is recommended for its large, round marble-like berries from October and throughout the winter
SH	Viburnum	Both *Viburnum fragrans* and V. *bodnantense* flower during mild spells in winter. V. *fragrans* has pale creamy-pink blossom and that of V. *bodnantense* is a brighter pink and the clusters are larger. Both are sweetly scented. Floral foam. Woody stem conditioning

Glossary

Abstract   A style of arrangement which uses plant material for its design qualities and not naturalistically.

Accessory   Anything other than plant material used as part of a show exhibit, though the container, base, background or drape are not usually considered to be accessories.

Base   A stand under the container.

Biennial   A plant that needs two growing seasons to complete its life cycle.

Bract   A modified leaf, often as colourful as a petal.

Calyx   The outer part of a flower which protects the petals and consists of sepals. It is usually green.

Conditioning   The term given to the treatment of flowers and foliage after cutting and before arranging.

Container   Used to be called vase and refers to anything into which flowers are put.

Design   A flower arrangement with or without accessories.

Design elements   The working qualities of colour, line, form, texture and space.

Design principles   The guidelines to the use of the elements: balance, rhythm, dominance, contrast, scale and proportion.

Exhibit   The term in the show schedule for the entire design.

Floral foam   One of the main mechanics for the flower arranger. There are two sorts of foam: green for soaking in water for fresh plant material and brown for dried and wired stems.

Floret   A small flower, part of a large head or cluster.

Foam holder   Similar to a pinholder but with only a few strong pins on which the foam is anchored. The best are made of lead and so give valuable base weight.

Focal point   An area of greater interest in an arrangement, usually near the centre of the design.

Frog   A small lightweight three- or four-pronged foam holder.

Garland   An elongated and flexible design that may be twined round a pillar, hung vertically or looped.

Half-hardy annual   A plant which completes its life cycle in one growing season but needs protection until frost danger is past.

Hardy annual   A plant that germinates, flowers and seeds in one growing season.

Hardy perennial   A plant that lives for an indefinite number of years. Not a tree or shrub.

Hogarth curve   The lazy S curve extolled by the artist William Hogarth (1697–1764) in his *Analysis of Beauty*.

Inflorescence   The arrangement of the flowers on the stem, e.g. a spike (lavender), umbel (allium), corymb (hydrangea), panicle (lilac) etc.

Interpretative design   An arrangement portraying a title. Plant material and other components all help to illustrate the theme.

Landscape   A design interpreting a natural scene, e.g. moorland, woodland, waterside, etc.

Mechanics   The various means by which stems are held in position.

Natural plant material   Either fresh or preserved material.

Pinholder   An indispensable mechanic – a Japanese-inspired, lead-based, brass-pinned stem holder.

Swag   A three-dimensional design of plant material assembled with no visible background.

Index